BLESSED
ARE THE
BORN
AGAIN

BLESSED ARE THE BORN AGAIN

R. KENT HUGHES

While this book is designed for your personal
enjoyment, it is also intended for group study.
A Leader's Guide with Victor Multiuse Transparency
Masters is available from your local bookstore
or from the publisher.

VICTOR BOOKS™

A DIVISION OF SCRIPTURE PRESS PUBLICATIONS INC.
USA CANADA ENGLAND

All Scripture quotations are from the *New American Standard Bible*, © the Lockman Foundation 1960, 1962, 1963, 1968, 1971, 1972, 1973, 1975, 1977.

Recommended Dewey Decimal Classification: 248.4
Suggested Subject Headings: CHRISTIAN LIFE; BIBLE. N.T. MATTHEW

Library of Congress Catalog Card Number: 86-60862
ISBN: 0-89693-369-5

VICTOR BOOKS A division of SP Publications, Inc. Wheaton, Illinois 60187

CONTENTS

To Barbara

as a grace note

for

twenty-five years

ONE.
ARE "EVANGELICALS" BORN AGAIN?

"There is a kind who is pure in his own eyes, yet is not washed"
(Prov. 30:12).

Are "Evangelicals" born again? This long-smoldering question was aflame again in my mind after the events of the last hour. For in the privacy of a convention hotel room, I had just witnessed an Evangelical leader come to Christ.

The hour had left me emotionally exhausted. I was initially incredulous as the man recounted his enviable heritage. He was the son of a prominent theologian and minister. From childhood he had attended Christian schools and had graduated from a Christian college. He had married a fine Christian from another notable family. His children were believers. He was successful in business, a leader in his denomination, and the board member of several prestigious Christian organizations.

My initial incredulity gave way to shock as he carefully explained that since his youth he had known that he was not a believer. Conforming to conventional piety had come easy to him. As a boy, he had "gone forward" and been baptized. He also knew his Bible and offered admirable prayers over dinner and in public.

Yet all the while he was perfectly aware, almost sardonically so, that he had never truly bent his knee to Christ—and was not born again.

Moreover, he explained that he would never have come for spiritual help if his illegal business practices had not been discovered. He had come to the end of himself. There was nowhere to turn but to Christ—and he did. As we knelt together, I witnessed a movingly passionate and genuine outpouring of contrition for sins. This man, this "Evangelical" leader, believed in Christ, repented, and was truly born again.

The Question Must Be Asked

"Are Evangelicals born again?" is much more than an attention-getting gimmick. It is a profoundly valid question which the newly arrived Evangelical establishment needs to ask itself.

By "Evangelical" we mean one who believes the Bible is divinely inspired and infallible, and who subscribes to doctrinal formulations which teach the depravity of man, the substitutionary death and atonement of Christ, salvation by unmerited grace through personal faith in Christ (not good works), the necessity of a transformed life, the existence of a literal heaven and hell, and the visible, personal return of Jesus Christ to set up His kingdom of righteousness. Moreover, he or she believes in the proclamation of the Gospel and the mission of winning the world for Christ.[1]

George Gallup's much-discussed religious survey of 1978 established one thing for certain: many Evangelicals are woefully ignorant of the Bible and do not maintain beliefs or live lives which are consonant with their Evangelical profession.[2] These realities alone ought to be cause enough for question.

Jesus Himself warns us in His Parable of the Wheat and the Tares (Matt. 13:24-30) that it is the enemy's practice to sow counterfeit believers among Christ's true followers, so perfectly disguised that they will not be discovered till the harvest.

It is apparent that many have fallen to what Dietrich Bonhoeffer memorably warns of as "cheap grace."

> Cheap grace is the preaching of forgiveness without requiring repentance, baptism without church discipline, Communion without confession, absolution

without personal confession. Cheap grace is grace without discipleship, grace without the cross, grace without Jesus Christ, living and incarnate.[3]

Today, the sad truth is, there are thousands of "Evangelicals" (Bible-carrying, church-attenders) who are not born again.

The Ease of Being Evangelical

The greatness of the problem is easily seen when we realize that it is not very difficult to be accorded the status of "Evangelical," whether born again or not. The process is essentially *cultural*. That is, display similar cultural traits and you will be accepted. Here are listed some of the most effective:

VOCABULARY. Biblical history records that when the Gileadites and the Ephraimites were warring, the Gileadites developed a password to detect Ephraimites who pretended to be Gileadites when captured. The word was *Shibboleth* which the Ephraimites (who had trouble with the *sh* sound) could only pronounce *Sibboleth*. It worked perfectly on the unsuspecting enemy (Jud. 12:4-7).

We Evangelicals have our Shibboleths, but unfortunately they are easy to pick up. They are words and phrases like *fellowship* and *brother* and *born again*. Use these passwords with the right inflection and you will fool most of the people most of the time.

SOCIAL CONVENTIONS. It is most effective to share the same social attitudes about alcohol and tobacco, modesty and style of clothing. Simply put, share the same likes and dislikes (especially dislikes) and you will probably pass as Evangelical.

The ease with which you can adopt the behavioral mores of Evangelical Christianity has been greased by the gradual alignment of many Evangelicals with the materialism, hedonism, and fads of our secular culture.[4]

HERITAGE. If your parents are respectable Christians, or even better, Christian workers, it will probably be assumed that you are a believer. And by attending evening service and prayer meeting and practicing the tithe you will place yourself beyond question.

The desire of overly anxious parents to see their children born again has contributed to this "heritage equals salvation" delusion. Some well-meaning parents have manipulated their children into bogus confessions, bogus baptisms, and bogus membership. Not a few of these offspring go on to be admitted to Christian schools on the basis of "testimonies" ghosted by their parents.

For these and similar reasons, multitudes of unregenerate "Evangelicals" are comfortably ensconced in their churches. And no one has the gracious temerity to question the authenticity of their faith.

The Attraction of Evangelicalism

Why would anyone ever willfully take up the "narrow way" of Evangelical Christianity apart from being born again?

A major reason has already been anticipated. For many it is the path of least resistance. To do otherwise would impair comfortable family and social relationships.

Besides, Evangelical Christianity has arrived. Though its arrival may be no more than an Indian summer,[5] its preachers dominate the religious media. Its recording artists sell big. A billion dollars is spent annually on its publications. It even makes and breaks politicians. Being "born again" can be profitable. Jesus saves, but Jesus also sells.

We must remember too that the biblical lifestyle is a good way to live. Families subscribing to biblical models tend to be happier and healthier and to stay together. It is not at all surprising that the wholesome, solid way of Christianity attracts those who would practice its style without knowing its inner reality.

The human race has an infinite capacity for self-delusion. And nowhere is it more perfectly demonstrated than in the lives of thousands of "Evangelicals" who are not born again.

What wise Solomon said of his day goes for ours as well: "There is a kind who is pure in his own eyes, yet is not washed from his filthiness" (Prov. 30:12). Jesus tells us that a terrible surprise awaits immense numbers of such "believers" at the judgment:

Many will say to Me on that day, "Lord, Lord, did we not prophesy in Your name, and in Your name cast out demons, and in Your name perform many miracles?" And then I will declare to them, "I never knew you; depart from Me, you who practice lawlessness" (Matt. 7:22-23).

John Newton, the 18th-century father of English Evangelicalism, provides this sobering dictum that is refreshingly humble and healthy:

If I ever reach heaven I expect to find three wonders there: first, to meet some I had not thought to see there; second to miss some I had thought to meet there; and third, the greatest wonder of all, to find myself there.[6]

The Beatitudes: A Beautiful Remedy

On that memorable morning when I was used by God to lead the Evangelical leader to Christ, I asked him to turn to the first Beatitude and read it aloud: "Blessed are the poor in spirit for theirs is the kingdom of heaven" (Matt. 5:3). It had an electrifying effect. He saw at once that he had never been poor in spirit, but proud and self-sufficient, and thus self-excluded from the kingdom. The truth of the first Beatitude penetrated him, broke him, and opened him to the grace of Christ.

This is what the Beatitudes do, for *they describe the inner character of those who are members of the kingdom of heaven.*

The careful reader will notice that the first and last Beatitudes begin and end with the same phrase—"for theirs is the kingdom of heaven." It is a Hebrew stylistic device called an *inclusion* which means that everything in the Beatitudes is about the kingdom of heaven.[7] I like to call the Beatitudes the "Beautiful Attitudes" for in them we see what the heart of a true child of God is like—the truly born-again heart.

Cultural tests are, of course, of some use in determining our spiritual state, but certainly fallible. Theological, confessional tests are far better. However, we can confess the creeds and not be born again. We can say we believe in Christ and yet really not believe. All unregenerate "Evangelicals" do!

But the Beatitudes are even more revealing of our spiritual state. They are functional tests of our spiritual life. If we are true believers, then *something* of each of the eight Beatitudes will be present in our lives. This is not to suggest that anyone can perfectly model the Beatitudes or be saved by living them, but rather that if one does not have something of each of the Beatitudes in his or her life—if the Beatitudes are not incipient and growing in one's life—that person may well not be born again.

Do we have the life of Christ and therefore the character of the kingdom? The Beatitudes will tell us.

There is nothing quite like them in all of Scripture. They are the opening lines of the greatest sermon ever preached. Their very position makes them seminal for life. They are absolutely crucial. As our Lord gives them to us as recorded in Matthew 5:3-12, they come with inexorable, hammerlike logic. One follows the other in a gracious aggression that not only reveals the true state of our hearts, but calls us to even higher plains of holy living.

On Taking the Medicine

The Beatitudes provide perfect medicine for Evangelicals. However, they are not to be applied by us to others. But though we dare not apply them to others, we dare not refrain from applying them to ourselves.

As you undergo the tests of the Beatitudes in each of the eight succeeding chapters, my prayer is that the Holy Spirit will cause you to see yourself in true, gracious light.

May those of you who are born-again Evangelicals be challenged to deeper authenticity as you grow in the character of the kingdom.

May those of you who are not—be born again.

NOTES

[1]R.V. Pierard, "Evangelicalism" in the *Evangelical Dictionary of Theology*, Walter A. Elwell, ed., Baker, 1984, p. 379. See also George Marsden, ed., *Evangelicalism and Modern America*, Eerdmans, 1984, pp. vii-xix.

[2]*Christianity Today*, "The Christianity Today-Gallup Poll: An Overview," December 21, 1979, vol. 23, no. 28, pp. 14-15.

[3]Dietrich Bonhoeffer, *The Cost of Discipleship*, Macmillan, 1969, p. 47.

[4]Os Guinness, *The Gravedigger File*, InterVarsity Press, 1983, pp. 130-139.

[5]Donald Bloesch, *Crumbling Foundations*, Zondervan, 1984, p. 91. "The striking resurgence of evangelicalism in America may be an Indian summer before the total collapse of organized religion in this country."

[6]Tryon Edwards, *The New Dictionary of Thoughts*, Classic Publishing House, 1931, p. 251.

[7]Donald Carson, *The Sermon on the Mount*, Baker, 1978, p. 16.

TWO.
THE POOR

"Blessed are the poor in spirit, for theirs is the kingdom of heaven" (Matt. 5:3).

Those of us who grew up in the Fifties are quite familiar with the name Mickey Cohen because he was the most flamboyant criminal of the day. Perhaps some of us even remember Cohen's becoming a "Christian."

The story goes like this. At the height of his career, Cohen was persuaded to attend an evangelistic service at which he showed an interest in Christianity. Hearing of this, and realizing what a great influence a converted Mickey Cohen could have for Christ, many prominent Christian leaders began visiting him in an effort to convince him to accept Christ. Late one night, after repeatedly being encouraged to open the door of his life on the basis of Revelation 3:20, "Behold, I stand at the door and knock; if anyone hears My voice and opens the door, I will come in," Cohen did so.

Hopes ran high among his believing acquaintances. But with the passing of time, no one could detect any change in Cohen's life. Finally, they confronted him with the fact that being a Christian meant that he would have to give up his friends and his profession. His logic was this: there are "Christian football players, Christian cowboys, Christian politicians; why not a Christian gangster?"[1]

What happened to Mickey Cohen dramatically underscores what is happening to untold numbers today. Though many ostensibly have "accepted Christ," they have not experienced the "poverty of spirit" which the first Beatitude (Matt. 5:3) tells us is characteristic of the kingdom of heaven.

What they need is exposure to the life-giving logic of its lines so that they can become what the Lord calls "blessed." And it is with this word that we begin.

Blessedness: The Approval of God

Each of the eight Beatitudes opens with "Blessed" and it is essential that we understand here in the beginning what this word means, for it bears on everything that will be said in the remainder of the book.

Contrary to popular opinion, *blessed* does not mean "happy" even though some translations render it this way. Happiness is a subjective state, a feeling. Here, Jesus is not declaring how people feel, but making an objective statement about what God thinks of them.[2] *Blessed* is a positive judgment by God on the individual which means "to be approved" or "to find approval." *So when God blesses us, He approves us.*[3]

Now there is no doubt that such blessing will bring feelings of happiness, and that blessed people are generally happy. But we must remember that the root idea of "blessed" is an awareness of approval by God. Blessedness is not simply a nice wish from God; it is a pronouncement of what we actually are—*approved*.

Do We Desire God's Approval?

As we begin this study of the Beatitudes, let us realize that if God's blessing/approval means more to us than anything else—even the approval of our friends, business acquaintances, and colleagues—then the Beatitudes are going to penetrate our hearts, speaking to us in the deepest of ways.

The question is, do we really want His approval more than anything else? Not do we want to be happy (certainly such a desire is OK), but, do we really want God's approval above all?

If this is what we want, then we must heed every word of the text, for it gives us the condition of blessing in just three words: "poor in spirit." "Blessed/approved are the poor in spirit."

It is so important to the understanding of the Beatitudes that we get off to a good start with the first one that I would like to suggest the following prayer. Will you pray it now?

> Lord Jesus, I want to be blessed in all of my spiritual life. I want Your smile on all aspects of my character. So make the Beatitudes come alive to me. Especially help me to understand what this first Beatitude means by "poor in spirit," then apply it in my life so that I can go on to understand and live the others—and know Your fullest blessing. Amen.

Understanding Poverty of Spirit

What does *poor in spirit* mean? Let us answer by first stating what it is not. *Poverty of spirit* is not the conviction that one is of no value whatsoever. It does not mean the absence of self-worth or as one theologian put it, "ontological insignificance." It does not require that we believe ourselves to be zeros. Such an attitude is not scriptural, for Christ's death on our behalf teaches us that we are of infinite value (1 Cor. 6:20; 7:23).

Neither does *poor in spirit* mean shyness. Some who are naturally shy and introverted are extremely proud. Nor does *poor in spirit* mean lacking in vitality, spiritually anemic, gutless. Certainly, *poor in spirit* does not refer to showy humility like Uriah Heep, in Charles Dickens' *David Copperfield,* who kept reminding people that he was a "very humble person."

Martyn Lloyd-Jones tells of meeting such a man on one of his preaching missions. When Lloyd-Jones arrived at the train station, the man asked for the minister's suitcase, and in fact, almost ripped it from his hand saying, "I am a deacon in the church where you are preaching tomorrow. . . . You know, I am a mere nobody, a very unimportant man, really. I do not count; I am not a great man in the church; I am just one of those men who carry the bag for the minister."

Lloyd-Jones observes, "He was anxious that I should know

what a humble man he was, how 'poor in spirit.' Yet by his anxiety to make it known, he was denying the very thing he was trying to establish. Uriah Heep—the man who thus, as it were, glories in his poverty of spirit and thereby proves he is not humble.''[4]

We all have met this kind of person, who by his own self-conscious diffidence is begging for us to say that he is not really nothing, but actually quite wonderful. When this attitude is present, there is an absence of poverty of spirit.

What, then, does *poor in spirit* mean? The history of the Greek word used here, *ptochos,* provides some insight. It comes from a verbal root which denotes "to cower and cringe like a beggar." In classical Greek *ptochos* came to mean "someone who crouches about, wretchedly begging."

In the New Testament, it bears something of this idea for it denotes a poverty so deep that the person must obtain his living by begging. He is fully dependent on the giving of others. He cannot survive without help from the outside. "Beggarly poor" is an excellent translation.

Now, if we take this meaning and combine it with the following words, *in spirit*, we have the idea: "Blessed are the *beggarly* poor in spirit." The sense is, "Blessed are those who are so beggarly poor in their spiritual resources that they realize that they must get help from outside sources."

Succinctly stated, "Poverty of spirit is the personal acknowledgment of spiritual bankruptcy."[5] It is the awareness and admission that we are utterly sinful and without the moral virtues adequate to commend us to God.

John Wesley put it this way, "He has a deep sense of the loathsome leprosy of sin which he brought with him from his mother's womb, which overspreads his whole soul, and totally corrupts every power and faculty thereof."[6]

It is the recognition of our personal moral unworth. The "poor in spirit" see themselves as spiritually needy. My favorite rendering of the verse is, *"Blessed are those who realize that they have nothing within themselves to commend them to God, for theirs is the kingdom of heaven."*

The World Rejects Poverty of Spirit

Poverty of spirit is the antithesis of the proud selfishness and self-sufficiency of today's world. The world has its own idea of blessedness. Blessed is the man who is always right. Blessed is the man who is strong. Blessed is the man who rules. Blessed is the man who is satisfied with himself. Blessed is the man who is rich. Blessed is the man who is popular.

Today's men and women think that the answer to life is found in self. Actress Shirley MacLaine says:

> The most pleasurable journey you take is through yourself. . . . The only sustaining love involvement is with yourself. . . . When you look back on your life and try to figure out where you have been and where you are going, when you look at your work, your love affairs, your marriages, your children, your pain, your happiness—when you examine all that closely, what you really find out is that the only person you really go to bed with is yourself. . . . The only thing you have is working to the consummation of your own identity. And that is what I have been trying to do all my life.[7]

Someday, if history is allowed to continue, a perceptive artist may sculpt a statue of 20th-century man, properly portraying him with his arms wrapped about himself in loving embrace, kissing his mirror image.

To this, Jesus answers, "Blessed (approved of God) are the poor in spirit, for theirs is the kingdom of God."

POVERTY OF SPIRIT IS ESSENTIAL FOR BLESSING. We must understand and embrace a true poverty of spirit for it is the only ground of divine blessing. David became the greatest king of Israel and the key to his rise to greatness was his poverty of spirit. Listen to his words when it all began, "Who am I, and what is my life or my father's family in Israel, that I should be the king's son-in-law?" (1 Sam. 18:18) Later in life, before his fall, he said, "Who am I, O Lord God, and what is my house, that Thou hast brought me this far?'' (2 Sam. 7:18)

Gideon, whom we celebrate for his amazing deliverance of Israel with just 300 men, began with these words, "O Lord, how shall I deliver Israel? Behold, my family is the least in Manasseh, and I am the youngest in my father's house" (Jud. 6:15).

POVERTY OF SPIRIT IS ESSENTIAL FOR SALVATION. Poverty of spirit is an indispensable sign of grace. No one can truly know Christ without it. There are most likely scores in your own community of Evangelicals, prominent "Christians" who do not know Christ.

There are tares amidst wheat who perhaps do not even know it (Matt. 13:24-30). They have never come to the blessed emptiness, to the very end of themselves. They have never confessed, "There is nothing in me to commend me to God," and thus they are lost.

No one can come to Christ without poverty of spirit. This is not to say that one must have a *perfect* sense of one's spiritual insufficiency to be saved. Very few, if any, come to this. Rather, it means that the spiritually proud and self-sufficient, those who actually think that there is something within them that will make God accept them—these people are lost.

Stated another way, "Those who acknowledge themselves as spiritually bankrupt enter the kingdom of heaven." No one enters God's kingdom without such an acknowledgment, regardless of how many times he has walked the aisle, raised a hand, signed a decision card, or given his testimony. Poverty of spirit is the posture of grace. God pours out His grace to the spiritually bankrupt, for they are open to receive His grace and salvation. He does this with no one else. No one can enter the kingdom without poverty of spirit.

POVERTY OF SPIRIT IS ESSENTIAL FOR SPIRITUAL GROWTH. Contrary to the thinking of some, we never outgrow the first Beatitude, even though it is the basis by which we ascend to the others. In fact, if we outgrow it, we have outgrown our Christianity—we are post-Christian.

That is what happened in Laodicea. Christ rebuked that failing church with these stern words:

> Because you say, "I am rich, and have become wealthy, and have need of nothing," . . . you do not know that you are wretched and miserable and poor and blind and naked. I advise you to buy from Me gold refined by fire, that you may become rich, and white garments, that you may clothe yourself, and that the shame of your nakedness may not be revealed; and eye-salve to anoint your eyes, that you may see (Rev. 3:17-18).

No one can come to Christ without poverty of spirit, and no one can continue to grow without an ongoing poverty of spirit.

Poverty of spirit is foundational because an ongoing poverty of spirit is the basis for ongoing spiritual blessing. An ongoing awareness of our spiritual insufficiency places us in the position of continually receiving spiritual riches. Poverty of spirit is something we never outgrow. In fact, the more spiritually mature we become, the more profound will be our sense of poverty.

It is because of this that every believer should commit the Beatitudes to memory and that the first Beatitude, especially, should become his or her conscious refrain, "Blessed are the beggarly poor in spirit." "Blessed are the spiritually bankrupt, for theirs is the kingdom of heaven."

The Reward for Poverty of Spirit

We have seen what the blessing/approval of God is and how it comes through poverty of spirit. Now we turn to the statement of the reward, "for theirs is tne kingdom of heaven." *Theirs* is emphatic. It means theirs in the sense of *theirs alone,* barring all others who approach God with a different spirit than that of beggarliness.[8] None but those who are poor in spirit will enter the kingdom of heaven.

The reward of the kingdom is both now and future. It is present because all who have life are in the kingdom now. We are seated with Christ in the heavenly places, *now* (Eph. 2). We are subjects of Christ, *now.* We are overcomers, *now.* We are a kingdom of priests, *now.*

What does this mean for today? It means we are kings and queens, and that we reign in life and exercise vast authority and power. It means that our "poverty of spirit," our weakness, is the reservoir of authority and power. Our weakness is the occasion for His power; our inadequacy for His adequacy; our poverty for His riches; our inarticulation for His articulation; our tentativeness for His confidence (see 2 Cor. 12:9-10; Col. 2:9-10).

As kings and queens, we are also free. Pride makes slaves out of all whom it possesses; not so with poverty of spirit. We are free to be full of God, free to be all that He would have us to be, free to be ourselves. What a marvelous reward! We reign now and for all eternity. The kingdom is ours—ours alone.

Some Abiding Lessons

What are the lessons of the first Beatitude? The greatest lesson of this Beatitude is that without poverty of spirit no one enters the kingdom of heaven—no one is saved. The prominent position of this Beatitude—spoken by Christ first of all—tells us that no one enters the kingdom of heaven who consciously and stubbornly imagines that there is something within him that will make God favor him.

Moral self-esteem, self-righteousness, vainglory will damn us! Jesus illustrated this with the story of the taxgatherer and the Pharisees:

> Two men went up into the temple to pray, one a Pharisee, and the other a taxgatherer. The Pharisee stood and was praying thus to himself, "God, I thank Thee that I am not like other people: swindlers, unjust, adulterers, or even like this taxgatherer. I fast twice a week; I pay tithes of all that I get." But the taxgatherer, standing some distance away, was even unwilling to lift up his eyes to heaven, but was beating his breast, saying, "God, be merciful to me, the sinner!" I tell you, this man went down to his house justified rather than the other; for everyone who

exalts himself shall be humbled, but he who humbles
himself shall be exalted (Luke 18:10-14).

We must realize that the initial tie between our souls and Christ
is not our goodness but our badness, not our merit but our
misery, not our standing but our falling, not our wealth but our
need.

Listen to Jesus' words, "Blessed (approved of God) are the
(beggarly) poor in spirit, for theirs is the kingdom of heaven
(now and forevermore)."

The question I must ask is, have you experienced true poverty
of spirit? Can you say,

> Nothing in my hand I bring,
> Simply to Thy cross I cling;
> Naked, come to Thee for dress
> Helpless, look to Thee for grace;
> Foul, I to the fountain fly;
> Wash me, Saviour, or I die.

Do you truly know Jesus? Or, are you a church attender
without Christ? Are you an unregenerate "Evangelical"? Are
you a Christless "Christian"? If so, hear God's Word and take it
to heart: "Blessed are the poor in spirit, for theirs is the kingdom
of heaven."

The other great lesson for all of us, regardless of spiritual
maturity, is that poverty of spirit is necessary for continuing
spiritual blessing.

I personally can say that the most profitable spiritual experiences of my life have come out of times of profound spiritual
poverty, times when God has brought me face to face with the
fact of my need; times when I once again realize there is nothing
within me to commend me to Him.

Sometimes He has done this through professional failure,
sometimes through intellectual shortcomings, sometimes through
social or family pressures. But, whatever the case, in Him my
bankruptcy has been the opening for His riches. And it can be

yours. "Blessed are the poor in spirit, for theirs is the kingdom of heaven." Lord, make us blessed!

NOTES

[1]Charles Colson, *Who Speaks for God?* Crossway, 1985, p. 153.

[2]John R.W. Stott, *The Message of the Sermon on the Mount,* InterVarsity Press, 1979, p. 33.

[3]D.A. Carson, *The Sermon on the Mount,* Baker, 1978, p. 16.

[4]D. Martyn Lloyd-Jones, *Studies in the Sermon on the Mount,* vol. 1, Eerdmans, 1959, p. 47.

[5]Carson, *Ibid.,* p. 17.

[6]Edward H. Sugden, ed., *John Wesley's Fifty-three Sermons,* Abingdon, 1983, pp. 231-232.

[7]Charles Colson, *Loving God,* Zondervan, 1983, p. 8.

[8]George L. Lawlor, *The Beatitudes Are for Today,* Baker, 1974, pp. 40-41.

THREE.
THE MOURNFUL

"Blessed are those who mourn, for they shall be comforted"
(Matt. 5:4).

Charles Colson, in his brilliant book of essays, *Who Speaks for God?* tells of watching a segment of television's "60 Minutes" in which host Mike Wallace interviewed Auschwitz survivor Yehiel Dinur, a principal witness at the Nuremburg war-crime trials.

During the interview, a film clip from Adolf Eichmann's 1961 trial was viewed which showed Dinur enter the courtroom and come face to face with Eichmann for the first time since being sent to Auschwitz almost twenty years earlier. Stopped cold, Dinur began to sob uncontrollably and then fainted while the presiding judge pounded his gavel for order.

"Was Dinur overcome by hatred? Fear? Horrid memories?" asks Colson, who answers:

> No; it was none of these. Rather, as Dinur explained to Wallace, all at once he realized Eichmann was not the godlike army officer who had sent so many to their deaths. This Eichmann was an ordinary man. "I was afraid about myself," said Dinur. "I saw that I am capable to do this. I am . . . exactly like he."

Wallace's subsequent summation of Dinur's terrible discovery—"Eichmann is in all of us"—is a horrifying statement; but it indeed captures the central truth about man's nature. For as a result of the Fall, sin is in each of us—not just the susceptibility to sin, but sin itself.[1]

Colson follows his penetrating observation with this question: why is it that today sin is so seldom written or preached about? The answer is in Dinur's dramatic collapse—for to truly confront the sin within us is a devastating experience. If sin were preached on, says Colson, many would flee their church pews never to return.[2]

The abiding fact is that man has always been in need of such an encounter. And to this end Jesus has given the second Beatitude, because it shows the necessity of truly facing one's sin.

So no one would miss the point, the Lord put it in the most striking language.

Truth Upside Down
When read apart from its context the second Beatitude is startling, "Blessed are those who mourn, for they shall be comforted" (Matt. 5:4). It is, of course, a paradox—and it is meant to grab us.

G.K. Chesterton once defined a paradox as "truth standing on its head calling for attention," and this is certainly true here. Jesus states one of the essential truths of life in such a way that it cries for all to come and take a good long look, a look that can bring life. "Blessed/approved are those who mourn."

The intimate connection of this second Beatitude with the first is beautiful and compelling. The first Beatitude, "Blessed are the poor in spirit," is primarily intellectual (those who understand that they are spiritual beggars are blessed); the second Beatitude, "Blessed are those who mourn," is its emotional counterpart. It naturally follows that when we see ourselves for what we are, our emotions will be stirred to mourning.

Again, as with the previous Beatitude, we cannot place enough stress on the importance of these spiritual truths as they relate to the Gospel. The Beatitudes are *not* the Gospel because they do not explicitly explain Christ's atoning death and resurrection and how one may receive Him. *But they are preparatory to the Gospel.*

The Beatitudes slay us that we may live. They hold us up against God's standards for the kingdom so that we can see our need and fly to Him. They cut through the delusions of formula Christianity and expose the shallowness of those who give all the "right" answers but who do not know Christ. They can do so for you.

The Blessed Paradox

To begin with, what does the paradoxical pronouncement, "Blessed are those who mourn," mean? In answer, let us first note what it does not mean.

Jesus does not mean, "Blessed are the grim, perpetually down, morose, cheerless Christians." Some believers have apparently interpreted it this way. Charles Haddon Spurgeon once remarked that some preachers he had known appeared to have their neckties twisted around their souls.[3] Robert Louis Stevenson must have known some preachers like that because he once wrote in his diary, "I've been to church today and am not depressed." Christ is not pronouncing a Beatitude on someone with a forlorn disposition.

Neither does Jesus mean, "Blessed are those who are mourning over the difficulties of life." The Bible does not say that mourning by itself is a blessed state. It is not blessed any more than laughter is. In fact, some mourning is cursed. For example, Amnon mourned because his lust was not fulfilled by Tamar (2 Sam. 13:2). Also, Ahab mourned because he did not have Naboth's vineyard (1 Kings 21:4).

IT IS MOURNING OVER PERSONAL SINS. The kind of mourning that Jesus pronounces blessed is a sorrow over sin. In this respect, mourning over life's difficulties can be the path to blessedness, as we finally are driven to mourning over our sins.

John Stott once surveyed his congregation at All Souls' Church in London and found that the majority had come to Christ when they had come to the end of their resources through personal difficulty.

King David provides us with an unforgettable example of what it is to mourn over our sins, recorded in Psalm 51. In verse 4, he expressed his sorrow for sinning against God, confessing, "Against Thee, Thee only, I have sinned, and done what is evil in Thy sight." Certainly he mourned his sin against Bathsheba and Uriah, but the ultimate sorrow was that it was against Holy God. Then in verse 5 he went further and expressed sorrow for his own sinful nature, "Behold, I was brought forth in iniquity, and in sin my mother conceived me." David's profound poverty of spirit welled up and overflowed in profound sorrow and mourning—and it was "blessed."

The question for us is, can we truly say by this understanding of mourning that we are blessed?

IT IS MOURNING OVER THE SINS OF THE WORLD. Such personal mourning is naturally expansive because one who truly mourns over his sins will also sorrow over the power and effects of sin in the world. David, at his best, mourned for the sins of others in Psalm 119:136, "My eyes shed streams of water, because they do not keep Thy Law." The great characteristic of Jeremiah, the Weeping Prophet, was that he wept for his people (Jer. 9:1; 13:17).

Of course, our Lord Jesus was also deeply grieved by sin in the world. His heart was like a spiritual seismograph registering the slightest tremors of the earth's pain and sorrow. No wonder some thought Jesus was Jeremiah returned from the grave (Matt. 16:14).

So now we begin to see the force of the brilliant paradox of the second Beatitude. The Lord Jesus has stood truth on its head, and it shouts for us to take notice and understand. "Blessed/approved are those who mourn (over sin, that is their own sin and the sin that poisons the world), for they shall be comforted." Christ shouts for our understanding. Blessed are we if we understand and put our understanding to work.

Mourning Is Not Popular

Mourning is definitely not in vogue today, despite its necessity for spiritual health. This is very important for us to see. However, before elaborating on this point, we must emphasize that humor and laughter are good and necessary for the believer. Solomon says that a merry heart acts as a good medicine (Prov. 17:22), and we have found it to be true. Oswald Sanders underlines the need for laughter in the church with these questions:

> Should we not see that lines of laughter about the eyes are just as much marks of faith as are the lines of care and seriousness? Is laughter pagan? We have already allowed too much that is good to be lost to the church and cast many pearls before swine. A church is in a bad way when it banishes laughter from the sanctuary and leaves it to the cabaret, the nightclub, and the toastmasters.[4]

Now, having said this, let me say again that the world despises sorrow so much that it has gone wild in its attempt to avoid it. Most people have structured their lives to maximize entertainment and amusement, to make life one big party. They try to laugh all the time. They laugh when there is no reason to laugh. In fact, they laugh when they ought to cry.

Solomon was right that a merry heart acts like a good medicine. But that does not mean that you cannot overdose! Much of our culture has overdosed on merriment.

Moreover, the world thinks mourners (those who mourn the course of the world; who mourn sin) are crazy. John Wesley said that they consider it " . . . to be more moping and melancholy, if not downright lunacy and distraction."[5] Some have actually argued that Martin Luther was insane because of his deep mourning over his sin before his new birth. They judged his behavior as psychotic. The world regards pain of heart with suspicion and restraint.

The church is much the same. Some suppose that if we are good Christians, filled with the Spirit, we will experience no sorrow, sporting eternal beatific smiles like plastic Mona Lisas, breaking into bubbly Christianese whenever we converse.

I personally know of some preachers who, though they maintain that they belong in the Evangelical tradition, never mention sin in their preaching because it makes people unhappy. The result is a Christianity which is as shallow as a birdbath—if indeed it is Christianity at all!

True Christianity is what we cry over and what we laugh about. So often we laugh at the things that we should weep over and weep over the things we should laugh about. What do we weep about? What do we laugh about?

Mourning Is Beneficial

What does all this mean personally? Simply this: in matters of spiritual life and spiritual health, mourning is not optional. Spiritual mourning is necessary for salvation. No one is truly a Christian who has not mourned over his sins. As you come to God, you cannot be forgiven if you are not sorry for your sins.

This was powerfully brought home in the article, "There Is One Thing Worse than Sin," which first appeared in the *Chicago Sun-Times,* August 22, 1983, by Thomas F. Roeser. In it, Dr. Roeser compared the equally reprehensible sins of Congressmen Daniel Crane and Gerald Studds. Both had been censured by the House of Representatives—Crane for having sexual relations with a seventeen-year-old female page and Studds for having relations with a seventeen-year-old male page. Roeser observes:

> Being censured is the only thing Crane and Studds have in common. The nation got a glimmer of their philosophical differences when Crane admitted tearfully to his district, then to the full House, that he "broke the laws of God and man," casting a vote for his own censure, facing the House as the Speaker announced the tally. Studds, in contrast, acknowledged he was gay in a dramatic speech to the House, then defended the relationship with the page as "mu-

tual and voluntary." He noted that he had abided by the age of consent, and said the relationship didn't warrant the "attention or action" of the House. Studds voted "present" on the censure and heard the verdict from the Speaker with his back to the House.

Roeser goes on to contrast and evaluate the different moral traditions both these men represent—properly excusing neither one his immense sin.

But [he concludes] there's one consolation for Crane. His . . . philosophy teaches that there is one thing worse than sin. That is denial of sin, which makes forgiveness impossible.[6]

The saddest thing in all creation is not a heart that sorrows, but a heart that is incapable of grief over sin, for that heart is without grace. Without poverty of spirit no one enters the kingdom of God. Likewise, without its emotional counterpart—grief over sin—no one receives the comfort of forgiveness and salvation.

Mourning Is Absolutely Essential

If you have never sorrowed over sin (not just its consequences, but sin itself) in your own life, then consider long and carefully whether you really are a Christian. True believers have mourned, and continue to mourn, over sin.

This brings us to the application of the principle to believers: ongoing mourning for sin is necessary for spiritual health. The tense of the verb for mourning is continuous. So for the godly, mourning is an ongoing process, a constant cry. Believers perpetually mourn, perpetually repent, and perpetually confess. Add to this the fact that of the nine verbs used in the New Testament for *mourning,* this is the most intensive. It is an intense, inward, though outwardly restrained, grief.[7]

It is significant that the first of Martin Luther's famous *95 Theses* states that the entire life is to be one of continuous repentance and contrition. It was this spirit in the Apostle

Paul that caused him to affirm, well along into his Christian life, that he was the chief of sinners (1 Tim. 1:15).

What is the result of our mourning? In the first Beatitude, we see that an ongoing poverty of spirit leaves us open to ongoing blessings of the kingdom. Here, our ongoing mourning opens us to His unspeakable comfort and joy.

This naturally anticipates and introduces the paradoxical reward, " . . . for they shall be comforted."

The Blessed Reward: Comfort

What about this comfort? Note that it is immediate. Don't be put off by the future tense. It is used with reference to mourning. The actual sense of Christ's words is, "Blessed now are the mourners, for they shall be immediately comforted, and they will continue to be so."

THE COMFORT OF FORGIVENESS. Notice, most of all, that the basis of our comfort is that we are forgiven. Believers are the only people in the world free from the guilt of their sins. The word *they* is emphatic: "they alone shall be comforted—no one else." We actually know we are mourners if we have a comforting sense of God's forgiveness.

This forgiveness is also accompanied by changed lives. The sources of so much personal sorrow—arrogance, judgmentalism, and the like—are changed as we mourn them and are forgiven. Therefore, comfort springs from within—from changed lives.

THE COMFORT OF THE HOLY SPIRIT. The very Greek word used here for *comfort* has the root from which we get *paraclete*, the One who comes alongside and comforts us. God's comfort is relational. It comes in the form of His divine companionship. He is our ally. He personally binds up our sorrows and comforts us.

How comprehensive our comfort is! It is immediate. It comes to us alone. It comes personally in the Person of the Holy Spirit. And it is based on the forgiveness of our sins. That is why we are called "blessed."

What a stupendous paradox. Jesus stands truth on its head to get our attention, and He says, "Would you be comforted? Then mourn. Would you be happy? Then weep."

THE COMFORT OF SALVATION. To those who are not yet believers, understand that this paradox is meant to lead you to salvation. If a spirit of mourning is welling within you, then ride your mourning to Him.

Do as the prodigal son did. He recognized his condition and mourned over it; and in the midst of his sin he said:

> I will get up and go to my father, and will say to him, "I am no longer worthy to be called your son; make me as one of your hired men." And he got up and came to his father. But while he was still a long way off, his father saw him, and felt compassion for him, and ran and embraced him, and kissed him (Luke 15:18-20).

Are you "poor in spirit"? Do you acknowledge that there is nothing within you to commend you to God? Are you mourning? Do you ache with the guilt of your sin before God and man? If so, come to Him now and He will give you the kingdom.

He will put His robe on your shoulders, His ring on your hand, and His sandals on your feet. You will be comforted!

That is what He has done for Charles Colson and multitudes of others. Colson says of his own experience,

> That night when I . . . sat alone at my car, my own sin—not just dirty politics, but the hatred and evil so deep within me—was thrust before my eyes, forcefully and painfully. For the first time in my life, I felt unclean, and worst of all, I could not escape. In those moments of clarity I found myself driven irresistibly into the arms of the living God.[8]

Charles Colson rode his mourning to God. And so can you. Be comforted now!

NOTES

[1]Charles Colson, *Who Speaks for God?* Crossway, 1985, pp. 136-137.

[2]Colson, *Ibid.,* p. 137.

[3]C.H. Spurgeon, *Lectures to My Students,* Zondervan, 1969, p. 166.

[4]Oswald Sanders, *Spiritual Leadership,* Moody, 1967, p. 60.

[5]Edward H. Sugden, ed., *John Wesley's Fifty-three Sermons,* Abingdon, p. 239.

[6]*Christianity Today,* November 11, 1983, pp. 82-83.

[7]George L. Lawlor, *The Beatitudes Are for Today,* Baker, 1974, pp. 40-41.

[8]Colson, *Ibid.,* p. 138.

FOUR.
THE GENTLE

"Blessed are the gentle, for they shall inherit the earth"
(Matt. 5:5).

Two men faced each other on the pavement before the governor's palace. One was Jesus Christ, the meekest Man who ever lived. The other was Pontius Pilate, a man of cosmic pride.

Jesus appeared the epitome of weakness, a poor Jew caught on the inexorable tides of Roman history, frail and impotent, a man destined to be obliterated from the earth. Pilate was the personification of Roman power. The tides of history were with him. As part of Rome, he was heir to the earth.

The two figures are the antipodes of a tragic paradox. Jesus Christ, the prisoner, was the free Man. He was in absolute control. Jesus, the meek, would inherit not only the earth, but the universe. Pilate, the governor, was the prisoner of his own pride. He could not even control his soul. He had no inheritance.

Jesus not only taught the paradox, "Blessed are the gentle, for they shall inherit the earth," He lived it.

Christ was master of the paradox. His teaching is salted with magnificent paradoxes like:

Last is first
Giving is receiving
Dying is living

Losing is finding
Least is greatest
Poor is rich
Weakness is strength
Serving is ruling

For Christ, paradoxes were an especially effective way of getting us to see spiritual truth, in this instance, "Blessed are the gentle (meek), for they shall inherit the earth" (Matt. 5:5).

The beauty of a paradox is that it grabs our attention because it does not sound right to the ear. In the case of Matthew 5:5, it seems better to say "Blessed are the proud, the intimidating, for they shall inherit the earth." Or perhaps, "Blessed are the meek, for they shall inherit heaven."

But the earth? That doesn't make any sense at all. Jesus teaches the survival not of the fittest but of the meekest. How in the world are the meek going to inherit anything? Life simply doesn't work that way. Such thinking runs counter to the laws of nature—and society. Just look at those who occupy the executive suites—the strong, self-sufficient, overbearing, proud, capable, aggressive, and ambitious. The world belongs to the "John Waynes." It belongs to those who sing:

Out of the night that covers me,
Black as the Pit from pole to pole,
I thank whatever gods may be
For my unconquerable soul.[1]

The last thing the average man wants to be known for is meekness.

It seems that Jesus has made a great mistake, but of course we know that our Lord never erred. Indeed this paradox provides an infallible law of life and a Beautiful Attitude for living and dying.

The Paradoxical Pronouncement

So to begin, what does the opening statement mean? More specifically, what does the word *gentle* or as many translations have it, *meek,* mean?

Notice first, that it doesn't mean weak. Meekness is not weakness. It doesn't denote cowardice or any of its parallel characteristics such as spinelessness, timidity, or the attitude of peace at any cost.

Neither does meekness suggest indecisiveness, wishy-washiness, or lack of confidence. Nor does meekness imply shyness or a withdrawn personality, as contrasted to an extrovert. Nor can meekness be reduced to mere niceness.

As we shall see, the meekness that Christ calls us to is not a natural quality, because He calls all Christians to it. Every Christian, regardless of his natural temperament, is commanded to be meek.

Having seen what *meekness* is not, we must note that its development in classical literature and the other usages in the New Testament confirm the popular translations of *meek* and *gentle.*

In classical Greek the word was used to describe tame animals, soothing medicine, a mild word, and a gentle breeze.[2] "It is a word with a caress in it."[3]

The New Testament bears the same sense. John Wycliffe translated the third Beatitude, "Blessed be mild men."[4] *Gentleness* and *meekness* are, indeed, caressing words.

The word also implies self-control. Aristotle said that it is the mean between excessive anger and excessive angerlessness. So the man who is meek is able to balance his anger. He controls it. Meekness/gentleness is strength under control.[5] The meek person is strong! He is gentle, meek, and mild, but he is in control. He is as strong as steel. This is as far as a study of the word alone can take us.

Jesus Is the Personification of Meekness

Jesus said of Himself, "I am gentle (meek) and humble in heart" (Matt. 11:29). As the Incarnation of meekness, He displayed it in two ways, both of which show His power.

In respect to His own person, He practiced neither retaliation nor vindictiveness. When He was mocked and spat upon, He answered nothing. As we have noted, when He was confronted by Pilate, He kept silent. When His friends betrayed Him and fled, He uttered no reproach. When Peter denied Him, Jesus restored him. When Judas came and kissed Him in Gethsemane, Jesus called him "friend." Jesus meant it. He was never insincere. When in the throes of death, He pleaded, "Father, forgive them, for they do not know what they are doing" (Luke 23:34). In all of this Jesus, meek and mild, was in control. He radiated power.

Yet, when it came to matters of faith and the welfare of others, Jesus lashed out. He rebuked the Pharisees' hardness of heart when He healed the man's withered hand on the Sabbath (Matt. 12:9-45). He was angered when His disciples tried to prevent little children from coming to Him (Mark 10:13-16). Jesus made a whip and drove the moneychangers from the temple (John 2:14-17). He called Peter "Satan" after the outspoken fisherman tried to deter Him from His heavenly mission (Matt. 16:21-23). All of this came from Jesus, the Incarnation of gentleness.

Now bringing it all together, we have an amazing picture. The one who is meek has a gentle spirit. Indeed, there is a caress about his presence. At the same time the meek person possesses immense strength and self-control, which he exhibits in extending love rather than retaliation against those who do him evil. He stands up fearlessly in defense of others or of the truth as the occasion arises.

Meekness Is Approved

Now, note this, and note it well. Jesus says in essence, "Blessed (approved) are the gentle. My blessing, My approval rests on them, and they shall inherit the earth." Are you blessed? Can you say, "God approves of me"?

We must understand that if we do not have the quality of gentleness in our lives, we are not part of the kingdom. Of course, no one perfectly displays meekness in his life. No one's life is a perpetual caress. No one completely rises above retaliation. Nevertheless, if the Beautiful Attitude of a gentle spirit is not at least imperfectly present in our lives we must take heed as to whether we are of the faith. The truth is, our proud spirits will never become meek unless we are born again. If we are born again, the meekness and gentleness of Jesus will be present in our lives and, though incipient, growing.

Note also that Galatians 5:23 lists gentleness as *a fruit* of the Spirit. Therefore, it is only present through *the work* of the Spirit.

The Paradoxical Reward

The reward for meekness is truly amazing: "They shall inherit the earth." Paradoxically, the gentle-spirited will inherit the earth.

The inspiration for this magnificent paradox is Psalm 37, where six times (vv. 9, 11, 18, 22, 29, 34) the Lord enjoins His people not to fret because of evil around them, and encourages the faithful that they will inherit the earth. The time is coming when, as fellow heirs with Christ (Rom. 8:17), we will reign with Him in His earthly kingdom. We will inherit the earth. We will even judge the world (1 Cor. 6:2). The paradox will be literally fulfilled, far beyond our wildest dreams.

But there is also a present inheritance and it is equally wonderful. It has to do with the psychology of ownership. There is a sense in which the rich and proud never possess anything. This was given classic illustration by one of the world's richest men when asked how much is enough money and he answered, "Just a little bit more." He was a poor man, owning everything, yet possessing nothing!

It is the meek who own the earth now, for when our mental attitude is free from the compulsion of "just a little more," when a gentle spirit caresses our approach to our rights, then we possess all. Izaak Walton put it this way:

> I could there sit quietly, and looking on the waters see fishes leaping at flies of several shapes and colors. Looking on the hills, I could behold them spotted with woods and groves. Looking down the meadows, I could see a boy gathering lilies and lady-smocks, and

there a girl cropping columbines and cowslips, all to
make garlands suitable to this present month of May.
As I thus sate, joying in mine own happy condition, I
did thankfully remember what my Saviour said, that
the meek possess the earth.[6]

The meek are the only ones who inherit the earth. The *they* in
"they shall inherit" is emphatic: *they alone, only they* shall
inherit the earth. Are you meek? Then you are very rich right
now; and 50 billion trillion years into eternity you will find it is
still literally true!

On Becoming Meek

There are four things we can do to acquire Christlike meekness:

First, we must realize that a gentle, caressing spirit is a gift of
the Holy Spirit (Gal. 5:23). Therefore, it comes only through
grace. We must cast ourselves on God, asking that He give us
life, making us His children, instilling in us a spirit of meekness.

Second, we must give close attention to the progression of
thought in the Beatitudes, for it provides us with a three-step
ladder to meekness. The initial step begins in the first Beatitude
(Matt. 5:3) with poverty of spirit, which comes from a true
knowledge of ourselves. We realize that there is nothing within
us that would commend us to God. We fall short. We need God.

In the next Beatitude (v. 4) we progress to mourning. We most
naturally lament our state of spiritual poverty. This mourning is
an enviable state because in it we are blessed and comforted.

Now, we should note that poverty of spirit and mourning are
negative. However, when true poverty of spirit and spiritual
mourning are present, they make way for the positive virtue of
meekness. In a sense, meekness is superior to the two preceding
states because it grows out of them. The process is all so natural,
so beautiful, and also quite supernatural!

Now, we must stop here and say to ourselves, "I see how the
progression works and I see that it comes by grace, but how can I
know when I am truly meek?" That is a good question! Martyn
Lloyd-Jones gave his congregation in Westminster Chapel the

answer, and I can say it no better. "The man who is truly meek is the man who is amazed that God and man can think of him as well as they do and treat him as well as they do."[7] The test as to whether we are truly meek is not whether we can say that we *are* poor sinners, but rather what we *do* when someone else calls us vile sinners. That is the test. Try it!

A third ingredient essential for a spirit of meekness is prayer. We see that it comes by grace. We understand the three-step progression. Therefore, we must pray for it. We cannot bestow it on ourselves.

Finally, a fourth element of developing a meek and gentle spirit is yoking ourselves to Jesus, for Jesus was the Incarnation of meekness. Our Lord said of Himself, "Take My yoke upon you, and learn from Me, for I am gentle and humble in heart; and you shall find rest for your souls. For My yoke is easy, and My load is light" (Matt. 11:29-30). Jesus promises us that if we yoke ourselves to Him, we will learn gentleness and humility.

In biblical times, a young ox was yoked to an older, experienced ox so that the older might train him to perform properly. By bearing the same yoke, the untrained ox learned the proper pace and how to heed the direction of the master. We learn by being yoked to Christ, as we surrender our lives to Him for direction.

The Need for Gentle Christians
We need to rise above superficial Christianity. None of us must imagine that because we have good manners and display the proper social conventions that we are fulfilling the meekness called for in this third Beatitude.

Evangelical passwords and civilities will not do it. God will not be impressed nor will the world. May the paradoxes of the Sermon on the Mount penetrate our beings and drive us to an ongoing poverty of spirit, ongoing mourning, and ongoing meekness.

We cannot afford *not* to have this happen! Those closest to us need to see positive spiritual reality in our lives, especially the paradox of Christian meekness. They need to see its strength, as we are willing to put it on the line for others and stand tall for truth when necessary. They need to see gentleness and a nonretaliatory spirit within us. And when they do, they will see Jesus. That is who the world really needs to see!

NOTES

[1]William Henley, "Invictus" in *The Home Book of Verse*, selected and arranged by Burton E. Stevenson, 9th edition, Henry Holt & Co., n.d., pp. 3500-3501.

[2]Colin Brown, *The New International Dictionary of New Testament Theology*, Zondervan, 1979, vol. 2, pp. 256-257.

[3]William Barclay, *A New Testament Wordbook*, Harper & Brothers, n.d., p. 103.

[4]M.R. Vincent, *Word Studies in the New Testament*, Associated Publishers and Authors, 1972, p. 30.

[5]Barclay, *Ibid.*, p. 104.

[6]Hugh Martin, *The Beatitudes*, Harper & Brothers, 1953, pp. 44-45.

[7]D. Martyn Lloyd-Jones, *Studies in the Sermon on the Mount*, Eerdmans, 1959, vol. 1, p. 69.

FIVE.
THE FAMISHED

"Blessed are those who hunger and thirst for righteousness, for they shall be satisfied" (Matt. 5:6).

There is no doubt today about the importance of our appetites and diets. Nutritionists have dramatized their importance by telling us that we are what we eat. The logic is if we eat too many doughnuts and cream puffs, we'll become walking doughnuts and cream puffs. And the argument is pretty sound if you don't apply it too literally.

In the nonmaterial realm of the mind and the spirit, "you are what you eat" is more exact. If you feed on violence, excitement, erotica, and materialism, you will eventually personify them. You will become what you eat.

I think we can accurately say that Elvis Presley never understood this. His life was a pitiful pursuit of materialism and sensuality. In Elvis' heyday, he earned between $5 and $6 million a year. It is estimated that he grossed $100 million in his first two years of stardom.

He had three jet airplanes, two Cadillacs, a Rolls-Royce, a Lincoln Continental, Buick and Chrysler station wagons, a Jeep, a dune buggy, a converted bus, and three motorcycles.

His favorite car was his 1960 Cadillac limousine. The top was covered with pearl-white Naugahyde. The body was sprayed with forty coats of a specially prepared paint that included crushed diamonds and fish scales. Nearly all the metal trim was plated with eighteen-karat gold.

Inside the car there were two gold-flake telephones, a gold vanity case containing a gold electric razor and gold hair clippers, an electric shoe buffer, a gold-plated television, a record player, amplifier, air conditioning, and a refrigerator that was capable of making ice in two minutes. He had everything.

Elvis' sensuality is legendary. Those familiar with his mental and physical state in the last months of his life tragically reveal that Elvis had become very much the victim of his appetites. He was what he had eaten—in the profoundest sense.

I have recalled Elvis Presley's tragic life to highlight the significance of the Lord's teaching in this fourth Beatitude, because in it He sets forth the menu and appetite which brings spiritual health: "Blessed are those who hunger and thirst for righteousness, for they shall be satisfied" (Matt. 5:6).

In this splendidly paradoxical sentence Jesus tells us what we ought to eat and how we must eat if we are to have spiritual health and ultimate satisfaction. Spiritual health comes from the heart attitude, the Beautiful Attitude of spiritual hunger. My hope is that as we partake of this Beatitude it will increase and sustain our spiritual hunger, for such hunger will bring us profound spiritual health.

A Healthy Hunger

Because Christ prescribes the intake of righteousness as essential to spiritual health and satisfaction, the logical question is: what is this righteousness? Some have supposed that it is the righteousness described in Romans which God reckons to the believer's account, sometimes called imputed righteousness (Rom. 1:17). However, while such righteousness is foundational to every believer's salvation, that is not what is meant here.

Others have wrongly supposed that this righteousness refers to the vindication of the poor and oppressed. Actually, however, this vindication is a residual benefit of the righteousness here described.

What, then, is its precise meaning? Scholars have come to recognize that *righteousness* here in Matthew means "a pattern of conformity to God's will." The word *righteousness* occurs only once in the other four Gospels—Luke 1:75. However, it occurs seven times in Matthew, including five times in the Sermon on the Mount.

This desire to live in conformity to God's will is expansive. It includes an increasing sense of need for God—to be like Him. To hunger and thirst for this righteousness means longing after the practical righteousness which the Beatitudes represent. The one who hungers and thirsts wants the character of the kingdom. He pants after the fruit of the Spirit. He wants God's will and all it entails.

It Is a Desperate Hungering
The fourth Beatitude is a call to pursue conformity to God's will and is stated in the extremest of terms, "Blessed are those who hunger and thirst." The words are remarkably intense in that they refer to the strongest of human impulses. The intensity of the expression is difficult for us to feel because if we are thirsty, all we have to do is turn the tap for cold, refreshing water; or if we are hungry, open the refrigerator.

However, to the average Palestinian, this expression was terribly alive because he was never far from the possibility of starvation or dehydration. It is not a pleasant picture. Jesus is not recommending a genteel desire for spiritual nourishment, but a starvation for righteousness, a desperate hungering to be conformed to God's will.

The expression is further intensified by the fact that it is durative, "Blessed are those who (continually) hunger and thirst (starve) for righteousness." King David, at his best, was like this. He walked with God as few mortals have. He wrote some of our favorite psalms about his lofty spiritual experiences. Yet he also wrote of his continual thirst and hunger: "O God, Thou art my God; I shall seek Thee earnestly; My soul thirsts for Thee, my flesh yearns for Thee, in a dry and weary land where there is no water" (Ps. 63:1). "As for me, I shall behold Thy face in righteousness; I will be satisfied with Thy likeness when I awake'' (Ps. 17:15).

This is the way it is for a healthy believer. He never has enough of God and righteousness. He is always hungry.

Such Hungering Repulses or Draws Us

No doubt the language of this Beatitude does not make sense to the secularist. Indeed, the language is too strong for some Christians. It rules out sleek, self-satisfied, halfhearted religion. In fact, hungering and thirsting for righteousness is the only approach it recognizes.

For some of us, Jesus' words may recall some buried, almost forgotten glimmer of past life when we first came to Christ and saw visions and dreamed dreams. We hungered and thirsted for righteousness. We welcomed opportunities for self-sacrifice and were willing to go for it all. But time blunted our desires and what we call "the realities of life" took over and our dreams were no more. And now we are content with a life of lesser, limited devotion.

Yet we have not quite forgotten the joy and warmth of earlier times and Jesus' words still stir us. If so, we should heed His call because we can be restored to what we were meant to be. We must hope that we will never be spiritually satisfied. We must pray that each decade of our lives will find us more thirsty for a life pleasing to God. Let us pray that the hunger never stops, that we never think we have arrived.

"Blessed are those who desperately hunger and thirst for righteousness," says our Lord.

Hungering People Know Christ

Jesus pronounces the spiritually famished "blessed" or approved. The underlying reason for His pronouncement is that such people are saved. Those who truly hunger and thirst know Christ. We cannot imagine a better test of the authenticity of one's faith than this. If this verse is to you one of the most sublime statements in Scripture, you can be sure you are a Christian. If not, you had better enter into careful soul analysis.

It is a gracious test, because each of us knows in his heart of hearts whether he really does long for God and His righteousness.

Do you hunger and thirst for His righteousness? If the Lord has given you a discontent, you are blessed. In fact, it is fitting to call yourself "blessed." Have the audacity to say, "My hunger and thirst is a blessing. I am blessed. Thank You, God."

A Hungerer's Reward

There is a further reason we are blessed, and that moves us to the second part of the Beatitude. We are blessed for we "shall be filled." This truth was anticipated by the Virgin Mary before Jesus' birth when she sang in the Magnificat, "He has filled the hungry with good things" (Luke 1:53).

The Beatitude is, of course, another attention-grabbing paradox. It suggests that those who continually hunger are satisfied. Yet how can one be hungry and satisfied at the same time? Or how can one be satisfied and know hunger? It can be stated in many ways. Satisfied, but never satisfied. Full, yet empty. Content, but discontent.

PARADOXICAL SATISFACTION. How does it work? A delightful episode in my life explains it quite well. Someone left a plate of brownies in the church office for the pastoral staff. I resisted temptation (for a minute or two!) and then poured myself a cup of coffee and retreated to my study, brownie in hand. When I bit in, I tasted the best brownie ever, for it was layered with caramel. I was "in heaven" with my brownie and cup of coffee. Moreover, I was completely satisfied—for about half an hour. Then I began to hunger and thirst for more brownies! And I ate a few more with the same effect. It was a sublime cycle.

So, there you have the idea. The paradox describes a spiritual cycle. The more one conforms to God's will, the more fulfilled and content one becomes. But that, in turn, spawns a greater discontent. Our hunger increases and intensifies in the very act of being satisfied.

Paul lived in the blessing of this paradox. He wrote to Timothy, "I know whom I have believed" (2 Tim. 1:12). Yet to the Philippians he expressed a profound longing for Christ, "that I may know Him, and the power of His resurrection and the fellowship of His sufferings, being conformed to His death" (Phil. 3:10). Paul knew Christ intimately, but the intimacy and satisfaction made him starve for more. Bernard of Clairvaux stated it perfectly in the hymn we often sing:

> We taste Thee, O Thou living Bread
> And long to feast upon Thee still
> We drink of Thee, the Fountainhead,
> And thirst our souls from Thee to fill.

COMPLETE SATISFACTION. This experience of being filled is completely satisfying. All that the world offers us are empty cups. We cannot quench our thirst from empty cups. That is why our text emphasizes that "they alone (who hunger and thirst) will be filled." No one can know anything of this satisfaction but a believer.

Many Scriptures attest to the satisfaction that Christ brings:

> But whoever drinks of the water that I shall give him shall never thirst; but the water that I shall give him shall become in him a well of water springing up to eternal life (John 4:14).

> Jesus said to them, "I am the bread of life; he who comes to Me shall not hunger, and he who believes in Me shall never thirst" (John 6:35).

> For He has satisfied the thirsty soul, and the hungry soul He has filled with what is good (Ps. 107:9).

ETERNAL SATISFACTION. The filling is not only for now, but for eternity. The image of a divine feast is used more than once by Jesus to illustrate the satisfactions of the kingdom. On one occasion Jesus told His disciples, "Just as My Father has granted Me a kingdom, I grant you that you may eat and drink at My table in My kingdom'' (Luke 22:29-30). Now that will be eternal satisfaction!

The bliss of what we have been describing is beyond words. We need to heed the words of Isaiah: "Ho! Everyone who thirsts, come to the waters; and you who have no money come, buy and eat. Come, buy wine and milk without money and without cost. Why do you spend money for what is not bread, and your wages for what does not satisfy? Listen carefully to Me, and eat what is good, and delight yourself in abundance" (Isa. 55:1-2). We need to believe Jesus' words: "But seek first His kingdom and His righteousness; and all these things shall be added to you" (Matt. 6:33).

God's Call: A Profound Hunger

Think of the force of this fourth Beatitude as we understand it: "Blessed is the man who desperately longs for righteousness (conformity to God's will) as a starving man does for food, and as a man who is dying of thirst longs for water; for that man will be completely satisfied!"

"You are what you eat" is not as simple as it may first appear. It is a profoundly esoteric phrase. The tragedy of our time is that the world is hungering and thirsting after sex and wealth, violence and excitement—and it is becoming increasingly sensual, materialistic, and dangerous. The church's tragedy is that many in her are seeking the same things—and their diets are making them as empty and helpless as the world.

We must remember that Jesus has given us the answer with His own menu and appetite. The main course is righteousness—conformity to His will. The method is desperation. We are to starve for righteousness—and pursue it with all that is in us. The result is profound satisfaction, now and eternally.

How Is the Appetite?

We all need appetites for righteousness, and we need to increase them. But how? The answer lies in the irresistible logic of the Beatitudes. We must begin with the first Beatitude, true poverty of spirit, realizing that there is nothing within us morally that commends us to God. We must affirm our spiritual bankruptcy.

Next, we must graduate to the second Beatitude, truly mourning our sins and sinful condition as well as the sin about us. Then, we must ascend to the third Beatitude, by allowing our spiritual bankruptcy and mourning to instill in us a truly meek and gentle spirit—of such reality that when others say we are sinners and there is nothing within us to make God accept us, we respond with gentle, powerful love.

Finally, as we live the logic of the Beatitudes, we will be able to do nothing but desperately hunger and thirst for righteousness—having as our goal to lead lives that are pleasing to Him.

There are few things more important than our spiritual appetites. We need to hear Jesus' words afresh: "If you knew the gift of God and who it is who says to you, 'Give Me a drink,' you would have asked Him, and He would have given you living water" (John 4:10).

The fifth Beatitude, found in Matthew 5:7, "Blessed are the merciful, for they shall receive mercy," is the perfect corrective for all those who are caught in bitterness.

If you have problems similar to the two unhappy brothers, this chapter could be your liberation.

The Meaning of Merciful

The basic idea of the Greek word for *merciful* is "to have mercy on, to give help to the wretched, to relieve the miserable." And the essential thought here is that mercy gives attention to those in misery. From this we make the important distinction between mercy and grace. *Grace* is shown to the undeserving; *mercy* is compassion to the miserable. Thus the synonym for *mercy* is *compassion.* However, mercy is not simply *feeling* compassion. Mercy exists when something is done to alleviate distress. Jesus made this perfectly clear when, after He told the Parable of the Good Samaritan, He asked His questioner,

> Which of these three do you think proved to be a neighbor to the man who fell into the robbers' hands? And he said, "The one who showed mercy toward him." And Jesus said to him, "Go and do the same" (Luke 10:36-37).

MERCY IS COMPASSION IN ACTION. We must never imagine that we are merciful because we *feel* compassionate toward someone in distress. Mercy means *active* goodwill. The story is told of the English preacher who happened across a friend whose horse had just been accidentally killed. While a crowd of onlookers expressed empty words of sympathy, the preacher stepped forward and said to the loudest sympathizer, "I am sorry five pounds. How much are you sorry?" And then he passed the hat. Mercy is compassion in action.

MERCY IS FORGIVING. The eminent New Testament scholar, Robert Guelich, has shown that especially in this Beatitude *merciful* describes one who forgives and pardons another who is in the wrong.[3] The supreme display of this forgiving aspect of mercy in Scripture is that of Joseph to his brothers. The only reason they had not murdered him as a boy was that as they were ready to perform the act, they saw an approaching caravan and decided to sell him into slavery instead. Years later, when Joseph had his guilty brothers literally "at his mercy," he showed them exactly that. There was *compassion* as he wept for their misery, and then met their needs. There was *forgiveness* as he restored them all to his grace, saying, "You meant evil against me, but God meant it for good" (Gen. 50:20).

The merciful person forgives. He remembers his own sin and God's mercy to him, and he understands the weakness of others. When we encounter a truly merciful person, we see something of God, because mercy is an attribute of God. W.E. Sangster experienced something of this quality in his own life, as he tells it:

> It was Christmas time in my home. One of my guests had come a couple of days early and saw me sending off the last of my Christmas cards. He was startled to see a certain name and address. "Surely, you are not sending a greeting card to him," he said. "Why not?" I asked. "But you remember," he began, "eighteen months ago. . . . " I remembered, then, the thing the man had publicly said about me, but I remembered also resolving at the time with God's help . . . to forget. And God has "made" me forget! I posted the card.[4]

I once had as my associate a man who was like this. On one particular occasion the name of someone came up who had grievously slandered him, and I said something derogatory about that person. But to my embarrassment, he began to quietly defend this person: "Life has been hard for him . . . we have no idea of the pressures he has been under . . . he has done a lot of good things too." My friend had compassion on the miserable person who had given him so much trouble, and from what I could tell, had forgiven him. How beautiful it was. Our text tells us what God thinks of this, "Blessed (approved) are the merciful." God says, "Such are the ones that I approve. Such are blessed."

They Shall Receive Mercy

The reason the merciful are blessed is that "they receive mercy." The word *they* in the phrase is emphatic: "Blessed are the merciful, for they (they alone) shall receive mercy." Other Scriptures teach the same idea. James says, "For judgment will be merciless to one who has shown no mercy" (James 2:13). Jesus Himself says, "For if you forgive men for their transgressions, your Heavenly Father will also forgive you. But if you do not forgive men, then your Father will not forgive your transgressions" (Matt. 6:14-15).

Some have completely missed the point here, supposing that this Beatitude teaches that one can merit God's mercy by performing acts of mercy. Such an idea is at complete variance with the rest of Scripture which teaches salvation by grace alone (Eph. 2:8-9). Moreover, if receiving God's forgiveness could only be merited by becoming forgiving, none of us would ever be truly forgiven, for none would ever absolutely meet this standard.

What the Beatitude means is that those who are truly God's children, and as such are objects of His mercy, will themselves be merciful, and will receive mercy in the end. Showing mercy is evidence that we have received mercy.

This interpretation suggests two very penetrating tests. The first is this: if we have no mercy toward those who are physically and economically in distress, we are not Christians. Notice I did not say we become Christians by showing mercy toward the unfortunate, but that we are not believers if we are unwilling to show mercy to them.

This is precisely the point of the Parable of the Good Samaritan. Jesus told the story to demonstrate that the religious establishment of His day did not fulfill the Great Shema—loving God with all one's might and one's neighbor as oneself (Luke 10:25-28). The fact that the priest and the Levite turned away from the needy man proved they did not love their neighbor as themselves; they thus failed to fulfill the Law and were lost. But the Samaritan's act of mercy showed him to be in accord with the Law and a true child of grace.

If we remain impassive or callous to human need and refuse to do anything about it, we need to take a good long look at ourselves and see if we really are believers. John says it best: "But whoever has the world's goods, and beholds his brother in need and closes his heart against him, how does the love of God abide in him?" (1 John 3:17) This is a test Evangelicals haven't liked. Today, I suspect there are some who would reject this test outright. If so, they are in great peril of soul. True belief is never to be divorced from attitude and action.

The second test involves the corresponding aspect of mercy—forgiveness. The test is this: if we will not exercise mercy in forgiveness, we are not Christians. I realize that it is a frightening thing to say that we cannot be truly forgiven unless we have forgiving spirits. But it is true, because when God's grace comes into our hearts it makes us merciful. We demonstrate whether we have been forgiven by whether or not we forgive. So the bottom line is this: if we refuse to be merciful, there is only one reason. And that is that we have never understood the grace of Christ. We are outside grace and we are unforgiven.

Jesus taught this in the Parable of the Unmerciful Slave (Matt. 18:21-35). The slave owed his master an immense sum—in today's currency, about 20 million dollars! The debt was impossible to repay, so he pleaded with his master who in turn had compassion on him and astonishingly forgave him the entire debt. Then incredibly, the wicked slave went out, found one of his fellow slaves who owed him about $2,000, and threw him in prison because he could not pay. When the other slaves found out and reported this injustice to their master, he summoned the wicked slave and said to him:

> "You wicked slave, I forgave you all that debt because you entreated me. Should you not also have had mercy on your fellow slave, even as I had mercy on

you?'' And his lord, moved with anger, handed him
over to his torturers until he should repay all that was
owed him. So shall My Heavenly Father also do to
you, if each of you does not forgive his brother from
your heart (Matt. 18:32-35).

These are hard, violent, surgical words. But they are merciful-
ly violent. The Lord here is speaking of and to the religious
person who can state all the answers, attends church, leads an
outwardly moral life, but holds a death grip on his grudges. This
person will not forgive his relatives for some infraction; he has
no desire to pardon his former business associate, no matter what
he does; he nourishes hatreds, cherishes animosities, revels in
malice. Such a person had better take an honest inventory of his
life to see if he really knows Jesus.

Here, some words of qualification are in order. The warning is
not for those who find that bitterness and hatred recur even
though they have forgiven the offender. The fact that you have
forgiven and continue to forgive is a sign of grace, despite the
ambivalences and imperfections of your forgiveness. The warning is for those who have no desire to forgive. These are in soul
danger. There may also be some who find forgiveness difficult
because they have been recently offended, and are still in such
emotional shock that they *cannot* properly respond. The warning
is not for these. It is for those who *will not* forgive. The overall
point is, if we are Christians, we can forgive and will forgive,
however imperfectly it may be. We cannot live like the miserable brothers who divided over a dollar bill.

On Forgiving
The late Corrie ten Boom recalled in her book, *The Hiding
Place,* the postwar meeting with a guard from Ravensbruck
concentration camp, where her sister had died and she herself
had been subjected to horrible indignities.

It was at a church service in Munich that I saw him,
the former S.S. man who had stood guard at the

shower room door in the processing center at Ravensbruck. He was the first of our actual jailers that I had seen since that time. And suddenly it was all there—the roomful of mocking men, the heaps of clothing, Betsie's pain-blanched face.

He came up to me as the church was emptying, beaming and bowing, "How grateful I am for your message, Fraulein," he said. "To think that, as you say, He has washed my sins away!"

His hand was thrust out to shake mine. And I, who had preached so often to the people in Bloemendaal the need to forgive, kept my hand at my side.

Even as the angry, vengeful thoughts boiled through me, I saw the sin of them. Jesus Christ had died for this man; was I going to ask for more? Lord Jesus, I prayed, forgive me and help me to forgive him.

I tried to smile, I struggled to raise my hand. I could not. I felt nothing, not the slightest spark of warmth or charity. And so again I breathed a silent prayer. Jesus, I cannot forgive him. Give me Your forgiveness.

As I took his hand the most incredible thing happened. From my shoulder along my arm and through my hand a current seemed to pass from me to him, while into my heart sprang a love for this stranger that almost overwhelmed me.[5]

I personally know that forgiveness is possible for the most grievous of crimes. When I was a young man, I was acquainted with a Christian who took in a troubled teenager and tried to help him. The boy brutally murdered this man's daughter and went on to spend his life in prison. Amazingly, my friend forgave him, visited him regularly in prison, and eventually led him to Christ.

Fellow believer, regardless of the wrong done to you, you can forgive. By God's grace, you can forgive the domestic wrong. By God's grace, you can forgive the professional wrong. For your soul's sake, you must.

When we began our study of the Beatitudes we observed that they were given to us so that we could ascertain two things: the authenticity and the health of our faith. In the searchlight of this Beatitude, "Blessed are the merciful, for they shall receive mercy," is your salvation authentic? *Are you merciful? Are you forgiving?* Or do you hold grudges as your treasured possessions?

If you sense a personal need to further develop a merciful spirit's active compassion and forgiveness, here are some specific suggestions to follow. *First, admit your need to God.* Pray words to this effect, "Father, I know Your mercy. I have been merciful at times. But God, I'm far from what You desire." *Second, read the Scriptures which have to do with mercy.* Regarding compassion, read Luke 10:30-37. Also read sections from the Minor Prophets, which begin with the Book of Hosea. They are full of teaching about compassion. Regarding forgiveness, read Matthew 18:21-35; 6:14-15; and Ephesians 2:1-5. *Third, get out and practice mercy.* Become involved with the hurting. By God's grace, forgive those who have wronged you. Be merciful! "Blessed are the merciful, for they shall receive mercy."

NOTES

[1]John R. Claypool, *The Preaching Event,* Word, 1980, p. 39.
[2]*Ibid.,* pp. 37-40.
[3]Robert Guelich, *The Sermon on the Mount,* Word, 1982, pp. 88-89.
[4]Haddon Robinson, *Biblical Preaching,* Baker, 1980, p. 150.
[5]Corrie ten Boom, *The Hiding Place,* Chosen Books, 1971, p. 215.

SEVEN.
THE PURE

"Blessed are the pure in heart, for they shall see God"
(Matt. 5:8).

On February 17, 1982, the *Chicago Sun-Times* carried a story originally printed in the *Los Angeles Times* about Anna Mae Pennica, a sixty-two-year-old woman who had been blind from birth. At age forty-seven, she married a man she met in a Braille class; and for the first fifteen years of their marriage he did the seeing for both of them until he completely lost his vision to retinitis pigmentosa. Mrs. Pennica had never seen the green of spring or the blue of a winter sky. Yet because she had grown up in a loving, supportive family, she never felt resentful about her handicap and always exuded a remarkably cheerful spirit.

Then in October 1981, Dr. Thomas Pettit of the Jules Stein Eye Institute of the University of California at Los Angeles performed surgery to remove the rare congenital cataracts from the lens of her left eye—and Mrs. Pennica saw for the first time, ever! The newspaper account does not record her initial response, but it does tell us that she found that everything was "so much bigger and brighter" than she ever imagined. While she immediately recognized her husband and others she had known well, other acquaintances were taller or shorter, heavier or skinnier than she had pictured them.

Since that day, Mrs. Pennica has hardly been able to wait to wake up in the morning, splash her eyes with water, put on her glasses, and enjoy the changing morning light. Her vision is almost 20/30—good enough to pass a driver's test!

Think how wonderful it must have been for Anna Mae Pennica when she looked for the first time at the faces she had only felt, or when she saw the kaleidoscope of a Pacific sunset, or a tree waving its branches, or a bird in flight. The gift of physical sight is wonderful. And the miracle of seeing for the first time can hardly be described.

A Greater Seeing
Yet there is a seeing which surpasses even this—and that is seeing God. The vision of God has always been regarded by God's people as the highest good. The reasoning is impeccable: since nothing is higher than God, seeing God must be the greatest joy one can experience. Thus, when we pass from this world and see the face of Christ, the joy of that first split second will transcend all the accumulated joys of life. It will be the highest good, the *summum bonum,* the greatest joy, beside which the wonderful story of Mrs. Pennica's "miracle" dulls in comparison.

This is what the sixth Beatitude is about—seeing God. "Blessed are the pure in heart, for they shall see God" (Matt. 5:8). Jesus' words tell us how to get 20/20 spiritual vision. If we want to see God, this is *the* great text.

The outline is as simple as the text. First, the Beatitude, "Blessed are the pure in heart," and then the benefit, "for they shall see God." The Beatitude and the benefit.

The Beatitude: "Blessed Are the Pure in Heart"
As we begin, we must ask what does "Blessed are the pure in heart" mean? Or more specifically, what does *pure* mean? The basic idea is to be clean or pure in the sense of not being mixed with anything else. William Barclay tells that the Greek word was used of clear water, sometimes of metals without alloy, sometimes of grain that had been winnowed (freed from the

mixture of other particles), and sometimes of feelings that are unmixed.[1] As it is used in our text, it carries the idea of free from every taint of evil.

We must keep this squarely in mind because it is normally supposed that "pure" as in "pure in heart" primarily refers to begin pure in mind regarding matters of sensuality. It certainly includes these matters. But the idea cannot be so limited, for it is far deeper and more searching than the sensual purity of the mind. Here in the sixth Beatitude it means a heart that does not bring mixed motives and divided loyalties to its relationship with God. It is a heart of singleness in devotion to God—pure, unmixed devotion. James refers to this idea when he says, "Purify your hearts, you double-minded" (James 4:8). That is, "Get rid of your mixed motives, your duplicity, your double-mindedness; be simple and pure in your devotion."

Negatively, we can picture this idea in everyday life if we reflect on those people who, after having been introduced to us, kept talking and smiling, while at the same time looking behind and around us at other people and things. They really were not interested in us; they only saw us as objects or a means for something they wanted. In the God-man relationship such behavior is anathema. Positively stated, "purity" then is represented in the words *focus, absorption, concentration, sincerity,* and *singleness.*

"Blessed are the pure" is a searching statement, because focusing on God with a singleness of heart is one of our biggest problems in 20th-century Christianity. Very few in this frenetic age are capable of the spiritual attention which this Beatitude calls for.

DEPTH OF DEVOTION. The depth of what is called for here is seen in the qualifying words, *in heart.* We are to be singly focused in heart on God. In the Bible, *heart* means more than just the mind—it means the mind, the emotions, and the will. It is the totality of our ability to think, feel, and decide. So *pure in heart* means that not only our minds, but our feelings and actions are to be concentrated singly on God. If our focus is merely intellectual, then we are not pure in heart. As Martyn Lloyd-

Jones paraphrases it, "Blessed are those who are pure, not only on the surface but in the center of their being and at the source of every activity."[2] It is a staggering requirement.

The depth of this heart requirement is further underlined by the realization that it is from the heart that all our human problems come. Jeremiah said, "The heart is more deceitful than all else and is desperately sick" (Jer. 17:9). Jesus said, "For out of the heart come evil thoughts, murders, adulteries, fornications, thefts, false witness, slanders" (Matt. 15:19). Again He said, "There is nothing outside the man which going into him can defile him; but the things which proceed out of the man are what defile the man . . . . For from within, out of the heart of men, proceed the evil thoughts" (Mark 7:15, 21). The Scriptures are conclusive. But none of us needs Scripture to know this; all we have to do is look into our own hearts of darkness, observing the mixed motives, the distractions, the divided loyalties, to know this is perfectly true. The dictum of Ivan Turgenev, the 19th-century Russian novelist, applies to us all: "I do not know what the heart of a bad man is like. But I do know what the heart of a good man is like. And it is terrible."

AN IMPOSSIBLE DEPTH. The pressing question is, therefore, how can we ever make it? This is an impossible character demand. This Beatitude—this Beautiful Attitude—is beyond our reach. Jesus is asking for perfection. At the end of the first section of the Sermon on the Mount, this is precisely what He says, "Therefore you are to be perfect, as your Heavenly Father is perfect" (Matt. 5:48). This drives us to despair, for none of us perfectly models any of the Beatitudes. None of us *perfectly* exhibits a poverty of spirit. None of us *perfectly* mourns our sins. None of us is *perfectly* humble and gentle. None of us *perfectly* thirsts. No one is *perfectly* pure in heart. Under the Old Testament economy no one could keep the Law—everyone failed; and these Beatitudes are even more impossible.

Then what are we to do? There is only one answer. We must cast ourselves on the grace of God and thus receive His radical renewal. We must ask Him to implant and nourish the character of the kingdom in our lives. If we do this, these qualities will root and grow within us, though we will never attain absolute perfection in this life.

If the character of the kingdom is not present, then we must question whether we are truly believers. Here, with the sixth Beatitude, "Blessed (approved) are the pure in heart," we must ask ourselves, "Do I know anything of single-hearted devotion to God? Do I focus on Him in devotion and concentration? Or, is my heart *always* other places?" The answers to these searching questions may indicate the authenticity of one's faith; or, if a believer, the state of one's spiritual health.

God demands a humanly impossible character, and then gives us the character by His grace. And with that He bestows a humanly impossible vision.

The Benefit: "For They Shall See God"

The Beatitude's sublime benefit is a vision of God Himself. Here, as in the preceding Beatitudes, the word *they* is emphatic: "for they (alone) shall see God." And, as with the other Beatitudes, the future is in *immediate* reference to what goes before. They will see God as they become pure in heart. Moreover, the seeing is continuous.

What this means is that it is possible to actually see God in this life—now. I think this is what blind and deaf Helen Keller meant when someone bluntly said to her, "Isn't it terrible to be blind?" To which she responded, "Better to be blind and see with your heart, than to have two good eyes and see nothing." She was speaking of spiritual vision. Perhaps if it were possible for her to have heard of Mrs. Pennica's miraculous operation, she would have said, "That is wonderful. But there is yet a better seeing."

SEEING GOD NOW. Believers see God now. Of course, they do not see Him in His total being, because that would be too much for them. However, they do see Him in many ways. That was, and is, my experience. Before I became a Christian, I won a Bible-reading contest, but the words meant nothing to me personally. Just a short time later when I met Christ, the Word of God came alive. I couldn't get enough. I even read at night with my flashlight! The Bible was living and I saw God in its pages.

Believers also see God in creation. Psalm 29 records that David watched a thunderstorm and saw God. Of thunder he says, "The voice of the Lord is upon the waters; the God of glory thunders, the Lord is over many waters. The voice of the Lord is powerful, the voice of the Lord is majestic" (vv. 3-4). When David saw the lightning, his response was, "The voice of the Lord hews out flames of fire" (v. 7). This seeing is the special possession of the believer. We see the footprints and the hand of God in nature.

Those of faith also see Him in the events of life—even difficulties. Job exclaimed after his varied experience of life, "I have heard of Thee by the hearing of the ear; but now my eye sees Thee" (Job 42:5).

SEEING MORE OF GOD. Practically speaking, this sixth Beatitude tells us that the purer our hearts become, the more we will see of God in this life. The more our hearts are focused on God, absorbed with Him, concentrated on His being, freed from distractions, sincere—*single*, the more we will see Him. As our hearts become purer, the more the Word lives, the more creation speaks. Even the adverse circumstances of life seem to sharpen our vision of God. Seeing God in this life is the *summum bonum*—the highest good, because those who see Him become more and more like Him. "But we all, with unveiled face beholding as in a mirror the glory of the Lord, are being transformed into the same image from glory to glory, just as from the Lord, the Spirit" (2 Cor. 3:18).

ULTIMATE SEEING. But there is even more to seeing God, for the pure in heart will one day see Him face to face. As we have said, in that split second of recognition, believers will experience more joy than the sum total of accumulated joys of a long life. Believers will behold the dazzling blaze of His being which has been, and is, the abiding fascination of angels. Scripture and reason demand that we understand that it will be the greatest event of our eternal existence—the *visio Dei*, the vision of God. We need to believe it! We need the faith and vision of Job who said, "I know that my Redeemer lives, and at the last He will take His stand on the earth. Even after my skin is destroyed, yet from my flesh I shall see God; whom I myself shall behold, and whom my eyes shall see and not another. My heart faints within me" (Job 19:25-27). Fainting hearts should be our reaction at the prospect of the vision of God.

Now think of the complete Beatitude, "Blessed (approved of God) are the pure in heart (those with a simple, unmixed heart for God), for they shall (continuously) see God (in life—and in eternity)." Have we experienced, do we know, a purity of heart, an unmixed devotion to God? This is not to suggest that this is our perfect experience at every moment. But rather, do we *ever* experience it? Moreover, is this singleness our desire? If not, listen closely, for the answer exists.

On Receiving Sight

The irony of Mrs. Pennica's "miracle" according to Dr. Pettit, was that "surgical techniques available as far back as the 1940s could have corrected her problem." Mrs. Pennica lived forty of her sixty-two sightless years needlessly blind! Hear this, and hear it well: the technique for curing spiritual blindness has existed for two millenniums. The procedure is radical, but it is simple, because God is the physician. You must be radically born again. To be pure in heart, you must be given a new heart.

When Jesus informed Nicodemus of this necessity, Nicodemus quite naturally questioned how it could be. Jesus answered, "That which is born of the flesh is flesh, and that which is born of the Spirit is spirit" (John 3:6), saying in effect, "That which is animal is animal, that which is vegetable is vegetable, and that which is of the Spirit is spirit. Nicodemus, it is radical indeed." Jesus explained how spiritual birth happens in these words, "Do not marvel that I said to you, 'You must be born again.' The wind blows where it wishes and you hear the sound of it, but do not know where it comes from and where it is going; so is everyone who is born of the Spirit" (John 3:7-8). That is to say, "Nicodemus, it is the work of the Holy Spirit. You see His work as you do not see the wind, but only its effects." To us He says, "Trust God's Word; believe that Jesus' death on the cross paid the penalty for your sins; and thereby receive a new, pure heart in place of your heart of darkness." It is a miracle. It is all of God. It is free. It is yours as you believe. Do you believe?

On Improving Sight
Believers, this text is also a call to develop and enhance the purity and singleness of our hearts. What can we do? What can *you* do?

First, be absolutely honest with God about your heart condition. Is your heart pure and unmixed in motives or is there a lack of spiritual concentration? Be honest with God in giving your answer.

Second, realize and acknowledge that only God can make your heart pure. This is not to suggest passivity. Paul tells us, "So then, my beloved, just as you have always obeyed, not as in my presence only, but now much more in my absence, work out your salvation with fear and trembling; for it is God who is at work in you, both to will and to work for His good pleasure" (Phil. 2:12-13). James says, "Draw near to God and He will draw near to you. Cleanse your hands, you sinners; and purify your hearts, you double-minded" (James 4:8). The biblical balance is: I must do everything I can and still realize that it is not enough; only God can make my heart pure.

Third, fill yourself with God's Word. In the Upper Room, Jesus told His disciples, "You are already clean because of the word which I have spoken to you" (John 15:3). Immersion and interaction with God's Word will purify.

Fourth, think about what you will be in eternity. Make that eternal promise a prominent aspect of your meditation. The Apostle John is very exact in telling us to do so:

> Beloved, now we are children of God, and it has not appeared as yet what we shall be. We know that, when He appears, we shall be like Him, because we shall see Him just as He is. And everyone who has this hope fixed on Him purifies himself, just as He is pure (1 John 3:2-3).

You and I are going to be transformed at the *visio Dei* into the likeness of Christ. This is the most stupendous thing we could ever be told! Can we dare believe it? If we truly do, there will follow a profound purity and singleness of heart. Jesus said, "Blessed are the pure in heart, for they shall see God."

NOTES

[1]William Barclay, *A New Testament Wordbook*, Harper, n.d., p. 69.
[2]D. Martyn Lloyd-Jones, *Studies in the Sermon on the Mount*, Eerdmans, 1959, vol. 2, p. 111.

EIGHT.
THE PEACEMAKERS

"Blessed are the peacemakers, for they shall be called sons of God" (Matt. 5:9).

Will and Ariel Durant in their famous book, *The Lessons of History,* begin the chapter on "History and War" with these words: "War is one of the constants of history, and has not diminished with civilization and democracy. In the last 3,421 years of recorded history only 268 have seen no war."[1] That is a chilling statement. And it would, no doubt, be even more chilling if the facts of *unrecorded* history could be known. War is the constant reality of life. Today, anyone old enough to understand what is being said on television knows that multiple wars are being fought at this very moment.

What is the solution? The proposed answers are many. Some are tongue-in-cheek, like the despairing rationale which the Durants put in the mouth of a fictitious general:

> States will unite in basic cooperation only when they
> are in common attacked from without. Perhaps . . .
> we may make contact with ambitious species on other
> planets or stars; soon thereafter there will be interplan-
> etary war. Then, and only then, will we of this earth
> be one.[2]

More seriously, some argue it is a necessity that one of the superpowers gain ascendancy over the rest (through battle no doubt!) and then war will be outlawed—a *Pax Romana* revived. Others say that the inhabitants of the world simply must come to the conclusion that war is unprofitable, and thus refuse to fight. You remember the old bumper sticker—"What if they had a war and nobody came?" Another suggestion, akin to this but more elevated, is that nations must challenge the evil precedents of history and live by the Golden Rule, as it is said that a Buddhist king once did.

This last idea touches on the solution but it doesn't go far enough. The answer to war is not simply a matter of "bootstrap ethics"; it is profoundly theological. What is needed is a radical change in the human race if there is to be peace. No one can live the Golden Rule by mere human will. No one can master even one of the Beatitudes in his own strength. Peace is impossible for the human race apart from a radical change in human nature.

All of which brings us to the theme of the seventh Beatitude: "Blessed are the peacemakers, for they shall be called sons of God" (Matt. 5:9). I am convinced that this Beatitude, understood, taken to heart, and applied by the Holy Spirit, cannot only bring inner peace to our troubled hearts but also make us instruments of peace—peacemakers. This Beautiful Attitude has the potential to give us peace within; make us peacemakers in the lives of those around us; and molders of peace in society at large.

Blessed Are the Peacemakers

Fundamental to understanding what Christ is saying is the precise meaning of the beautiful word *peacemaker*. Taking the first half of the word, *peace*, we understand it to mean much the same as the Hebrew word *shalom*, which bears the idea of wholeness and overall well-being. When a Jew said *shalom*, he was wishing another more than the absence of trouble, but all that made for a complete, whole life. God's peace is not narrowly defined; it is much more than the absence of strife; it encompasses all of the person; it is positive.

The second half of the word, *makers*, demands that we understand that the person is not passive but a producer of peace. As it is used here, it is a dynamic word bursting with energy. Both parts of the word *peacemaker,* taken together, describe one who actively pursues peace in its fullness. He pursues more than the absence of conflict; he pursues wholeness and well-being.

Bearing this in mind, we can clearly see what a peacemaker is not. A peacemaker is not, as is commonly supposed, the kind of person who is easygoing and *laissez-faire,* the kind of person who does not care what anybody else does as long as it does not directly affect him. Ironically, our strife-ridden culture has idealized this type of person as a peacemaker, one who is content to just "patch things up," gloss over the issues, act as if everything is OK when it is not. Nor is the peacemaker an appeaser—the kind who wants "peace at any price." Appeasement doesn't make for peace. It just puts off the conflict. The history of Europe during the 1930s is the cosmic example of this. The peacemaker, contrary to what most people think, is not afraid of making waves.

What a Peacemaker Is
What then is a peacemaker like? To begin with, *he is characterized by honesty.* If there is a problem, he admits it. The Prophet Ezekiel warned against those who act as if everything is all right when it is not, who say " 'Peace!' when there is no peace" (Ezek. 13:10). Such individuals, according to Ezekiel, are merely plastering over cracked walls. The plaster obscures the cracks, but when the rain comes, the true state of the walls is revealed and the walls fall (vv. 10-11). Jeremiah, using some of the same phrasing, put it memorably, "And they have healed the wound of my people slightly, saying, 'Peace, peace.' But there is no peace" (Jer. 6:14). The peacemaker doesn't do this. He is painfully honest about the true status of peace in the world, in the society in which he moves, and in his own personal relationships. He admits failed relationships. He admits that he is at odds with others if it is so. He honestly acknowledges if others have something against him. He does not pretend that things are as they are not. He refuses to say, "Peace, peace!" when there is

no peace. He admits the cracks.

How this speaks to our condition. All of us tend to putty over the cracks. I think that this is particularly a male tendency. Even in our most intimate relationships, we tend to act as if everything is OK when it is not. We tend to avoid reality because we want peace, when, in fact, our avoidance heals the wound only slightly and prepares the way for greater trouble.

Next, a peacemaker is willing to risk pain. Any time one attempts to bring peace societally or personally, one risks misunderstanding and failure. If we have been wrong, there is the pain of apologizing. Or, on the other hand, we may have to endure the equally difficult pain of rebuking another. In any event, the peacemaker has to be willing to "risk it." It is so much easier to let things slide. It is far easier to rationalize that trying to bring true peace will only make things worse.

These two qualities of the peacemaker—honesty about the true status of peace and willingness to risk pain in pursuing peace— beautifully anticipate the next quality which is the paradox: *the peacemaker is a fighter.* To make the paradox even more striking, the peacemaker is a troublemaker. He makes trouble to make peace. He wages peace.

In accord with this, the Scriptures enjoin the aggressive pursuit of peace, telling us to be "diligent to preserve the unity of the Spirit in the bond of peace" (Eph. 4:3), and to "pursue the things which make for peace and the building up of one another" (Rom. 14:19). "If possible, so far as it depends on you, be at peace with all men" (Rom. 12:18). St. Francis of Assisi understood this call to the active pursuit of peace, as his prayer so beautifully recalls:

> Lord, make me an instrument of Thy peace.
> Where there is hate, may I bring love;
> Where offense, may I bring pardon;
> May I bring union in place of discord.

Because the peacemaker is a fighter, it does not suggest that he has a "license to kill." He can never be thoughtless or pugnacious. Rather his character and personality are permeated with the shalom of God. He is gentle. James wrote, "But the wisdom from above is first pure, then peaceable, gentle, reasonable, full of mercy and good fruits, unwavering, without hypocrisy. And the seed whose fruit is righteousness is sown in peace by those who make peace" (James 3:17-18). The peacemaker is positive, not negative. He is tolerant in the best sense of the word. He realizes we are all of fallen stock and so does not demand perfection of others. He is humble. His ego is in hand. And he is loving.

How beautiful true peacemakers are. Filled with peace themselves, they are honest about the state of the relationships around them. They are honest about what is in their own hearts and sensitive to where others are. They refuse to be satisfied with cheap peace. They refuse to say "peace, peace" when there is none. They are willing to risk pain and misunderstanding to make things right. Peacemakers will even fight for peace. Do you know people like this? Perhaps you're married to a peacemaker—and you've not seen his or her persistence as a virtue. Have you ever had an employee who was a peacemaker? If so, you have been very privileged. How beautiful they are because they are like Jesus.

The Ultimate Peacemaker

Our Lord Himself is, of course, the supreme Peacemaker. What we should see, as His life is held up as an example, is that there was nothing cheap about His peacemaking. The Apostle Paul wrote, "For it was the Father's good pleasure for all the fullness to dwell in Him, and through Him to reconcile all things to Himself, having *made peace* through the blood of His cross" (Col. 1:19-20, italics added). Christ saw the gravity of our problem and He refused to sweep it under the rug. Only a drastic solution would suffice, and so He "made peace" (the same root words as in Matthew 5:9!) *through His blood*. Christ is our supreme example of aggressiveness and sacrifice in bringing peace.

He also became the source of peace among all men.

> But now in Christ Jesus you who formerly were far off have been brought near by the blood of Christ. For He Himself is our peace, who made both groups into one, and broke down the barrier of the dividing wall, by abolishing in His flesh the enmity, which is the Law of commandments contained in ordinances, that in Himself He might make the two into one new man, thus establishing peace, and might reconcile them both in one body to God through the cross, by it having put to death the enmity. And He came and preached peace to you who were far away, and peace to those who were near (Eph. 2:13-17).

By His becoming "our peace," He thus dispenses His shalom in our hearts, enabling us to promote in each other everything that makes for well-being. The cost of this enabling power is beyond computation. It was, "with precious blood, as of a lamb unblemished and spotless, the blood of Christ" (1 Peter 1:19).

Jesus not only made possible peace with God and peace among men, He gave us the example of how a peacemaker goes about His work.

> Do nothing from selfishness or empty conceit, but with humility of mind let each of you regard one another as more important than himself; do not merely look out for your own personal interests, but also for the interests of others. Have this attitude in yourselves which was also in Christ Jesus, who although He existed in the form of God, did not regard equality with God a thing to be grasped, but emptied Himself, taking the form of a bondservant, and being made in the likeness of men. And being found in appearance as a man, He humbled Himself by becoming obedient to the point of death (Phil. 2:3-8).

In obtaining our peace, our Lord didn't grasp His glory and dignity, but instead He humbled Himself. The example stands for us who are called to "peacemaking." It is expensive! It costs to make peace. It may be humbling. Peacemakers are willing to lower themselves, to even lose their dignity to bring shalom to life. This is the way peacemakers always have been, and always will be.

A Radical Call

As we consider how this biblical truth applies to our lives, we cannot place enough emphasis on the radicalness of the call to be peacemakers. Peacemaking, as called for by Jesus, is not a natural human quality. It is above human nature. It is impossible. I never cease to wonder that this Beatitude is a favorite text of those who know little about Christianity. Secularists and pacifists love to quote Matthew 5:9 along with Isaiah 2:4, "They will hammer their swords into plowshares, and their spears into pruning hooks. Nation will not lift up sword against nation, and never again will they learn war." They even use it in books and on the sides of buildings and monuments. They say that this and the other Beatitudes are the real Gospel. If only men would practice them, the world would be renewed. They are correct, of course, as far as they go. For if the Beautiful Attitudes really were practiced, war would be no more. However, they cannot be practiced without a radical change in the heart and the radical enabling of the Holy Spirit.

The radicalness of Christ's call to peacemaking demands a radical remaking of human personality. One must first have a profound experience of the shalom of God. No one can become a peacemaker until he has found peace himself. The tragedy of our time is that people do not go to the heart of the matter. Without grace, we are natural enemies of God and of one another. Our hearts must be changed. When they are, and His peace permeates our lives, then we can be peacemakers. We can give only what we have.

This radical change coupled with a complete dependence on the Holy Spirit is what makes a peacemaker. The Holy Spirit molds the character of our lives so that our ethos is gentle, humble, and loving. The Holy Spirit enlightens our integrity so that we can honestly evaluate the development of peace in our personal lives and society. He enables us *not* to say there is peace when there is no peace. The Holy Spirit leads us to risk pain and misunderstanding as we make peace. He also leads us in developing a divinely aggressive spirit which even fights for peace. We need the radical work of Christ!

For They Shall Be Called Sons of God

Now, let us consider the benefits, the sublime benefits: "they shall be called sons of God." The precise meaning of this takes our hearts up to the heavenlies. Again, as in the six previous Beatitudes, the pronoun is emphatic. The Greek word order is "for they sons of God shall be called." The idea is they, and no others, shall be called God's sons. Moreover, the passive indicates that it is God, not mere man, who does the calling. God assigns the title.

The sublimity of this promise comes from the fact that the title, "sons of God," refers to character. The peacemaker partakes of the character of God. He is like God in the way he lives. No wonder God says, "Blessed are the peacemakers." The proper question to ask next is, what title does God assign to *us?*

Are We Peacemakers?

If we are not peacemakers, but instead are troublemakers, there is every likelihood that we are not true children of God. Peacemakers are sometimes troublemakers to bring peace, but troublemakers make trouble for the sake of trouble. If our character is such that we spread rumors and gossip about others; if we are constantly fomenting discontent; if we find joy in the report of trouble and scandal; if we are omnicritical, always faultfinding; if we are unwilling to be involved in peacemaking; if we are mean—if these negative qualities characterize our lives, there is a good chance we are not Christians. Notice I did not say, if we fall into these things or are struggling to control them; but rather if these elements are a part of our character. If this is what we are like, then we need to take a day off from work or school and spend it with the Scriptures open before us, seeking the face of God. True children of God are not troublemakers!

Before we end this study, some words on the "hows" of being a peacemaker. As we first saw, a peacemaker must experience the peace of God himself. The futility of attempting to make peace when our inner lives are walking civil wars has already been mentioned. We can impart only that which we possess. If we are believers, but have receded from the fullness of God's shalom, we must come to Him honestly and ask for a fresh implanting of His peace.

Then, we must remember that this seventh Beatitude is the last Beatitude which describes the *character* of the Christian, and that all the other Beatitudes build up to it. God's peacemakers are matured by passing through the experiences of the previous Beatitudes.

Beatitude One:	They have experienced poverty of spirit (the recognition that there is nothing within them to commend them to God) many times. In fact, it remains their ongoing awareness, and as such, is the ground for ongoing spiritual blessing.
Beatitude Two:	They have come face to face with their own sin and the world's sin. They have mourned over it—and the more they see, the more they mourn.
Beatitude Three:	Because of the authenticity of their poverty of spirit and mourning, they experience gentleness and humility in dealing with others.
Beatitude Four:	Because they have experienced poverty of spirit and mourning and meekness, they in turn have hungered and thirsted for all righteousness.

Beatitude Five: The reality of their own need has made them merciful and compassionate to others.

Beatitude Six: They have traveled through these experiences many times and have developed a purity or singleness of heart and have been blessed with a vision of God.

Beatitude Seven: And, finally having been so prepared, they are ready to go into the world to make peace. The energy of Christ flows through them.

Peacemakers are those through whom the entire Beatitudes course again and again—sometimes in order, sometimes out of order, sometimes only one, sometimes all together. Those with the Beautiful Attitudes—they are the peacemakers.

NOTES

[1]Will and Ariel Durant, *The Lessons of History,* Simon and Schuster, 1968, p. 81.
[2]*Ibid.,* p. 86.

NINE.
THE PERSECUTED

"Blessed are those who have been persecuted for the sake of righteousness, for theirs is the kingdom of heaven" (Matt. 5:10).

Some time ago I came across a poem by William Blake which, for me, was very moving, so I committed it to memory. The opening lines go like this:

> Joy and woe are woven fine,
> A clothing for the soul divine,
> Under every grief and pine
> Runs a joy with silken twine.[1]

Blake says that joy and woe are part of the fabric of life which God weaves and lovingly fits as perfect clothing for His children. It is mysterious and paradoxical. But there is great comfort in the fact that God is the weaver.

As we now take up the final Beatitude we find a sister paradox which is equally mysterious—for it involves the relationship of persecution and joy. To read this Beatitude for the first time is shocking. Think of hearing these lines for the first time ever:

> Blessed are those who have been persecuted for the
> sake of righteousness, for theirs is the kingdom of
> heaven. Blessed are you when men revile you, and

persecute you, and say all kinds of evil against you
falsely, on account of Me. Rejoice, and be glad, for
your reward in heaven is great, for so they persecuted
the prophets who were before you (Matt. 5:10-12).

Matthew Henry, the Puritan commentator, believed that the
reason Christ repeated Himself was because the statement was so
incredible. And he is probably right. Also, until now all the
Beatitudes have been given in the third person, "Blessed are
those," and that is the way this Beatitude begins; but the
repetition in verse 11 changes to the direct address of the second
person, "Blessed are *you* when men cast insults at *you*, and
persecute *you*" (italics added). The repetition of the Beatitude,
its personalization, and its position at the end of the list tell us
that it is of supreme importance for individual living and for the
church universal. Moreover, it occupies a prominent place in the
experience of the church because joy and persecution have
repeatedly been woven into a garment of praise to God.

Joy in Prison
Supernatural joy amidst trial has been the repeated experience of
the church. When Peter and the other apostles were flogged
before the Sanhedrin in those early days after Pentecost, "they
went on their way from the presence of the Council, rejoicing
that they had been considered worthy to suffer shame for His
name" (Acts 5:41). They experienced supernatural joy in
persecution.

Samuel Rutherford, the saintly Scottish pastor, wrote from his
filthy prison sty, "I never knew by my nine years of preaching
so much of Christ's love, as He taught me in Aberdeen by six
months imprisonment." "Christ's cross," he said, "is such a
burden as sails are to a ship or wings to a bird."[2] Rutherford's
joy was supernatural.

And, in our own time, a Romanian pastor describes how he
was imprisoned and tortured mercilessly and yet experienced
supernatural joy. Locked in solitary confinement, he had been
summoned by his captors, who cut chunks of flesh from his

body, and returned to his cell where he was starved. Yet in the midst of this sadistic treatment, there were times when the joy of Christ would so overcome him, that he would pull himself erect and shuffle about the cell in dance. So great was his joy that on release from prison and return to his home, he chose to fast the first day in memorial to the joy he had known amidst the impossible persecution of prison.

Hearing stories like these, we naturally ask how it is possible. How is it possible for one to know joy amidst persecution? Notice we do not say, how does one *enjoy* persecution? That is the wrong question. To suggest that one should enjoy persecution is to suggest a perversion.

The question is, how can we experience joy in persecution? In answer, we must realize that persecution of itself is neither blessed nor joyous. However, there is a kind of persecution which has God's blessing and results in the believer's joy.

The Persecution that Brings Joy

IT IS NOT SIMPLY PERSECUTION. Notice that the Beatitude doesn't say, "Blessed are the persecuted, period!" Unfortunately, this is the way it is sometimes read. And those who read it like this delude themselves into thinking that any time they experience conflict they are bearing the reproach of Christ. They often develop a "martyr spirit" and promote trouble for themselves, feeding the fantasy that they are superior Christians.

Joseph Bayly's satire, *The Gospel Blimp,* humors the point home. As the story goes, some believers in a small town who wanted to share their faith decided to employ what they called a Gospel Blimp. The blimp was repeatedly sailed across town, dragging banners and dropping tracts in backyards. At first the town put up with the idea, but the tolerance changed to hostility when the owners installed a loudspeaker and began showering the people with Gospel broadcasts. Finally, the populace had had enough, and the local newspaper ran an editorial:

> For some weeks now our metropolis has been treated
> to the spectacle of a blimp with an advertising sign

attached at the rear. This sign does not plug cigarettes
or a bottled beverage, but the religious beliefs of a
particular group in our midst. The people of our city
are notably broad-minded, and they have good-
naturedly submitted to this attempt to proselyte. But
last night a new refinement (some would say debase-
ment) was introduced. We refer, of course, to the
airborne sound truck, that invader of our privacy, that
raucous destroyer of communal peace.[3]

That night the Gospel Blimp was sabotaged, and, of course, the
Christians saw it as "persecution."

The point is, Christians are very often persecuted, not for their
Christianity but for lack of it. Sometimes believers are rejected
simply because they have lousy personalities. They are rude,
insensitive, thoughtless—and generally obnoxious. And the rejection they experience has nothing at all to do with Christ. Some
believers are rejected because they are discerned as proud and
judgmental. Such a spirit mixed with conventional piety is too
much for the nonchurched and churched alike. Some are disliked
because they are lazy and irresponsible. Incompetence mixed
with piety is sure to be rejected. Rejection and opposition are not
signs of blessing by themselves.

IT IS PERSECUTION FOR RIGHTEOUSNESS. Christ's words must
be read in their entirety. "Blessed are those who have been
persecuted for the sake of righteousness." And what righteousness is this? In context, it is the righteousness taught in the seven
preceding Beatitudes. The world cannot tolerate such a life.

First, poverty of spirit runs counter to the pride of the unbe-
lieving heart. Those who are admired by the world are the self-
sufficient, those who need nothing else; the supermen, not the
poor in spirit.

Second, the mourning, repentant heart that despises its own
sin and the sins of others is not appreciated by the world.

Third, the gentle and meek person, the one who has the
strength not to take up a personal offense is regarded as weak by
those without Christ. "Meek is weak" is the proverb of the day.

Fourth, hungering and thirsting for the spiritual, for Christ, is foreign and repugnant to a world that lusts after only those things which it can touch and taste.

Fifth, the truly merciful person who not only feels compassion and forgiveness, but gives it, is out of step with the grudge-bearing, callousness of the age. This person is an awkward, embarrassing rebuke to the uncaring.

Sixth, the pure, single-minded heart for God provides a shaming contrast to a hypocritical, ulterior-motivated culture.

Seventh, the peacemaker is hated because he will not settle for a cheap peace. All seven of these characteristics are intolerable to the world; and to the degree that one fulfills the Beatitudes, one will be persecuted. A righteous life will not make one popular!

IT IS PERSECUTION FOR CHRIST. The foundational reason why such a person will be persecuted is that he or she is like Christ. This is Jesus' point when He completes verse 11 with "on account of Me" instead of "for the sake of righteousness," used in verse 10. Everyone who lives like Jesus will be persecuted. There will be no escape. Listen to Jesus' testimony in John 15:18-20:

> If the world hates you, you know that it has hated Me before it hated you. If you were of the world, the world would love its own; but because you are not of the world, but I chose you out of the world, therefore the world hates you. Remember the word that I said to you, "A slave is not greater than his master." If they persecuted Me, they will also persecute you; if they kept My word, they will keep yours also.

Jesus tells us that if the wind was in His face, it will be in ours. Hear Paul's advice to Timothy, "And indeed, all who desire to live godly in Christ Jesus will be persecuted" (2 Tim. 3:12). Paul warned the Thessalonians, "For you yourselves know that we have been destined for this. For indeed when we were with you, we kept telling you in advance that we were going to suffer affliction; and so it came to pass, as you know" (1 Thes. 3:3-4). And he told the Christians in Antioch the same thing, "Through many tribulations we must enter the kingdom of God" (Acts 14:22). "Friends," he in essence said to the Galatian believers, "it has always been this way. When we live for Christ we will be persecuted" (Gal. 4:29).

Few people who have lived in our time have understood and expressed this better than Dietrich Bonhoeffer:

> Suffering, then, is the badge of true discipleship. The disciple is not above his master. . . . That is why Luther reckoned suffering among the marks of the true church, and one of the memoranda drawn up in preparation for the Augsburg Confession similarly defines the church as the community of those "who are persecuted and martyred for the Gospel's sake." . . . Discipleship means allegiance to the suffering Christ, and it is therefore not at all surprising that Christians should be called upon to suffer. In fact, it is a joy and a token of His grace.⁴

At one time in Charles Spurgeon's life when he was depressed and discouraged by the criticism being heaped upon him, his wife took a sheet of paper, printed on it in large, old English style the words of the eighth Beatitude, and tacked it to the ceiling over his bed. She wanted the reality to saturate his mind morning and evening: everyone who lives righteously will be persecuted! There are no exceptions.

How Do We Measure Up?

Such a compelling conclusion is a gracious call to examine the reality and health of our own faith. The logic is impeccable: since the first seven Beatitudes describe the character of the true believer, we must conclude that ostracism, persecution, and rejection are just as much signs of the believer as being poor in spirit or merciful. We should not be surprised when persecution comes, but rather, surprised when it does not. If the person who claims to follow Christ never experiences any persecution at all, it may be reasonably asked if he really is a Christian.

If we have never been rejected for sharing the Gospel of the kingdom, are we citizens of the kingdom? If we have not been out of step with the surrounding culture, and suffered its disapproval because we practice the ethics of God's children, are we truly God's children? These are merciful questions because they can only be answered with a yes or no. A simple answer will reveal the simple truth.

A word of caution. We should be careful not to condemn ourselves if, at the moment, we are not undergoing persecution. No one is persecuted all the time. Along with this, we must be careful not to imagine persecution in overly dramatic terms. Most of it is mundane, and some is even quite "civilized."

The Nature of Persecution

What is persecution like? The word rendered *persecute* in Matthew 5:10 bears the root idea of "pursue" or "chase." A good translation might be *harass*. "Blessed are the harassed." The restatement of the Beatitude in verse 11 amplifies this idea: "Blessed are you when men cast insults at you, and persecute you, and say all kinds of evil against you falsely." This casting of insults means literally "to cast in one's teeth," so that the sense here is of throwing things up in one's face. Sometimes persecution will go to physical extremes as the church's bloody history records, but most often it is verbal, sometimes audible, sometimes whispered, sometimes direct, sometimes venomous innuendo.

And we should note, and note it well, that nonviolent persecution can be just as difficult to bear as violent persecution. Verbal abuse and social ostracism may call for as much heroism as braving the arena. Some examples of what believers endure are: the conscientious worker who has given twenty years of faithful, hardworking service at his or her desk, and has been passed over again and again because the top brass are uncomfortable with that person's ethics; the warm and friendly student who is purposely excluded from conversation because he does not rub-

ber-stamp all that is said; the housewife who is considered dull
by her neighbors because she doesn't indulge in their social
practices. We could go on, but suffice it to say that indifference
and condescension can sometimes be harder to take than physical
violence.

The Real Tragedy of Persecution

These are all hard things to endure. But the tragedy today is not
that they happen to believers, but that very often, they do not.
Why? One reason is that some of us are cut off from the world.
We go to a church which is 100 percent Christian, attend Bible
studies that are 100 percent Christian, attend Christian schools,
exercise with believers, garden with believers, golf with believers—and thus experience no persecution. Others keep their
Christianity secret so as not to make waves with non-Christian
associates. The obvious problem here is that hidden Christianity
is probably not Christianity.

But by far the greatest reason there is so little persecution is
that the church has become like the world. If we want to get
along, the formula is simple. Approve of the world's morals and
ethics—at least outwardly. Live like the world lives. Laugh at its
humor; immerse yourself in its entertainment; smile benignly
when God is mocked. Above all, do not share your faith. Act as
if all religions converge on the same road. Don't mention hell.
Draw no moral judgments. Take no stand on the moral-political
issues. Follow this formula and it will be smooth sailing. It's
really quite easy.

However, the fact is the church must be persecuted or it is no
church at all. People need to be told that if they follow Christ,
there will be a price to pay. It will affect how they get along at
school. It will affect their profile at the club. It will affect how
they make their living.

The early church had no doubt about where a believer's duty
lay. About a hundred years after Jesus preached the Sermon on
the Mount, a man came to the great church father Tertullian with
a problem—his business interests and Christianity conflicted. He
ended by saying, "What can I do? I must live!" Tertullian

replied, "Must you?" When it came to loyalty to Christ and living, the real Christian chose Christ.[5] We must allow Christ to affect all of life.

It is a glorious thing when the church and the individual are persecuted for righteousness' sake because that means they are like Christ, and that Christ is closer than ever.

The Joy of Persecution

Persecution is a glorious thing because it is the persecuted who know great joy. In Matthew 5:12 Christ, the persecuted, said "Rejoice, and be glad, for your reward in heaven is great, for so they persecuted the prophets who were before you." We ought to rejoice in the fact that we keep "classy" company with the likes of the prophets. That is indeed a great honor!

But the primary source of our rejoicing is our reward, for Jesus says, "your reward in heaven is great." When John D. Rockefeller died, the public became immensely curious about how much he left behind. One man, determined to find out, secured an appointment with one of Rockefeller's highest aides. He asked the aide how much Rockefeller left behind and the man answered, "He left it all." Not so for those who have been persecuted for the sake of righteousness. The reward is "great," the Greek word *polus*, which means "immeasurably great."

God will not permit what has been done for His glory to go unrewarded. Listen to Paul's assurances: "For momentary, light affliction is producing for us an eternal weight of glory far beyond all comparison" (2 Cor. 4:17). "I have fought the good fight, I have finished the course, I have kept the faith; in the future there is laid up for me the crown of righteousness, which the Lord, the righteous Judge, will award to me on that day; and not only to me, but also to all who have loved His appearing" (2 Tim. 4:7-8).

All this brings compounded joy. It causes a Romanian pastor to lift his emaciated body and dance about his cell. It brings another to say, "My persecutions are as sails to a ship or wings to a bird." How so? Perhaps it is because persecution makes the present awareness of one's possession of the kingdom more vivid and joyous. Those who are persecuted really own the kingdom now. For the godly, persecution brightens and confirms hope— and so trials have a mystic sweetness.

Why else do we rejoice? Because we are commanded to. Jesus says, "Rejoice, and be glad," and the Greek connotes the idea, "Keep on rejoicing and keep on being glad."

With this, we complete our study of the Beatitudes. Now we have our Lord's composite description of a kingdom heart. It is a heart which is:

> Poor in spirit
> Mournful over sin
> Gentle/meek
> Merciful
> Pure
> Peacemaking
> Persecuted

This is what Jesus approves of. Of this heart He says, "Blessed." May we be blessed indeed!

NOTES

[1] William Blake, "The Auguries of Innocence" (lines 59-62), *The Complete Poetry and Prose of William Blake,* revised edition, David V. Erdman, ed., University of California Press, 1982, p. 491.

[2] Hugh Martin, *The Beatitudes,* Harper & Brothers, 1953, p. 75.

[3] Joseph Bayly, *The Gospel Blimp,* Windward Press, 1969, p. 32.

[4] Dietrich Bonhoeffer, *The Cost of Discipleship*, Macmillan, 1969, pp. 100-101.

BECOMING
BLESSED

The study of the Beatitudes undresses our inner man. They mirror what is actually within. Martyn Lloyd-Jones put it this way in *Studies in the Sermon on the Mount:*

> They really tell us everything about our Christian profession. And if I dislike this kind of thing, if I am impatient with testing, it simply means that my position is entirely contrary to that of the New Testament man. But if I feel, on the other hand, that though these things do search and hurt me, it is good for me to be humbled, and that it is a good thing for me to be held face to face with this mirror, which not only shows me what I am, but what I am in the light of God's pattern for the Christian man, then I have a right to be hopeful about my state and condition.

Perhaps now, having come this far in the book, you have seen yourself as you really are. On the most elementary level, you see yourself as either a Christian or a non-Christian. And hopefully, you have been moved by the desire to improve your state. If an unbeliever, you want to be born again, to be pronounced "blessed," and then to experience the reality of the Beatitudes. If a believer, you want to grow in grace so that more and more of the Beautiful Attitudes are in you.

If you are an unbeliever, or a believer seeking to lead someone to Christ, the following two chapters are for you. The first chapter, entitled "The Healed," provides an amazing illustration of what is involved in salvation. The second, entitled "The Receivers," gives the unfailing formula for growing in the character of the kingdom.

TEN.
THE HEALED

"And when He had come down from the mountain, great multitudes followed Him. And behold, a leper came to Him, and bowed down to Him, saying, 'Lord, if You are willing, You can make me clean.' And He stretched out His hand and touched him, saying, 'I am willing; be cleansed.' And immediately his leprosy was cleansed" (Matt. 8:1-3).

When Jesus finished giving the Beatitudes, He went on to explain in the remainder of the Sermon on the Mount how a person who had the Beautiful Attitudes of the kingdom lived in the world.

It was the greatest sermon ever preached and our Lord did not want the teaching to be wasted on His hearers. So He arranged for a living illustration of what is necessary to enter the kingdom. It was an illustration they would never forget, for it was the healing of a leper.

A Man in Need of Christ's Touch

The poor man was terribly ill. Dr. Luke, in the parallel account (Luke 5:12), describes him as "full of leprosy." So we must understand that the disease had run its course. None of us needs a detailed description of the poor man's loathsome, lionized appearance. If you've seen just one picture of someone full of leprosy, one picture is enough.

What is important to note is that leprosy, or Hansen's disease as it is better known today (after the man who diagnosed its cause), is not a rotting infection as is commonly thought, nor are its horrible outward physical deformities directly imposed by the disease. In recent years, the research of Dr. Paul Brand and others has proven that the disfigurement associated with Hansen's disease comes solely because the body's warning system of pain is destroyed. The disease acts as an anesthetic, bringing numbness to the extremities as well as to the ears, eyes, and nose. The devastation that follows comes from such incidents as reaching one's hand into a charcoal fire to retrieve a dropped potato, or washing one's face with scalding water, or gripping a tool so tightly that the hands become traumatized and eventually stumplike.[1]

Dr. Brand calls the disease a "painless hell," and well it is. The poor man in our story had not been able to feel for years, and his body, mutilated from head to foot, was foul and rotting.

THE LEPER WAS AN OUTCAST. In Israel the lot of a poor leper is summed up in Leviticus 13:45-46:

> His clothes shall be torn, and the hair of his head shall
> be uncovered, and he shall cover his mustache and cry
> "Unclean! Unclean!" He shall remain unclean all the
> days during which he has the infection; he is unclean.
> He shall live alone; his dwelling shall be outside the
> camp.

We can hardly imagine the humiliation and isolation of a leper's life. He was ostracized from society because it was thought at that time that leprosy was highly contagious (which it is not). He had to assume a disheveled appearance and cry "Unclean! Unclean!" whenever he came in range of the normal population. Lepers were typically beggars. There was little else they could do.

By Jesus' time, rabbinical teaching, with its absurd strictures, had made matters even worse. If a leper even stuck his head inside a house, it was pronounced unclean. It was illegal to greet a leper. Lepers had to remain at least 100 cubits away if they were upwind, and four cubits if downwind. Josephus, the famous Jewish historian, summed it up saying that lepers were treated "as if they were, in effect, dead men."[2]

THE LEPER REPRESENTED SIN. If this were not bad enough, it was also thought that those who had leprosy had contracted it because of some great personal sin. People jumped to this erroneous conclusion because in past history such people as Miriam (Num. 12:6-10), Uzziah (2 Chron. 26:19), and Gehazi (2 Kings 5:25-27) had been judged with leprosy.

Yet the plight of the leper was illustrative of the effects of sin, even though the leper was not any more sinful than anyone else. R.C. Trench, the great Greek scholar and the inspiration for, and first editor of, the monumental *Oxford English Dictionary*, recognized this: saying that though the leper was not worse or guiltier than his fellow Jews, nevertheless he was a parable of sin—an "outward and visible sign of innermost spiritual corruption."[3] The leper is then a physical illustration of ourselves apart from the cleansing work of Christ. For if we could see ourselves with spiritual eyes, apart from Christ, we would be forms of walking death—trying to cover ourselves with filthy rags.

Now, looking back to our text, as Christ descends the mountain, we must see that His meeting the leper was no chance encounter. The entire meeting was divinely choreographed. We have not the Sermon on the Mount, but the *Sermon on the Move* as He authenticates and illustrates His message. And from the perspective of the leper (our perspective!), we see what is involved in obtaining and experiencing the healing touch of Christ. These three brief verses tell us how to obtain and experience Jesus' touch.

Obtaining the Healing Touch of Christ

The vast throng that had attended Jesus' teaching descended the slope en masse. But suddenly the crowd halted. Matthew wrote, "And behold (and look!), a leper came to Him" (Matt. 8:2). No doubt the din of the multitude in descent was very considerable. But, above it, with increasing clarity, was heard the faint, "Unclean! Unclean!" As if the prow of a boat were moving through the throng, the leper steadily made his way to Jesus as the people fell back, fearing contamination. Perhaps some cursed him, but he kept coming until he was almost to Jesus, crying the refrain of his pitiful life, "Unclean! Unclean!" The Master was face to face with a foul, decaying leper, "full of leprosy" from head to toe.

AWARENESS OF SIN. And in this we see the first and fundamental qualification for obtaining the healing touch of Jesus: an awareness of one's condition. The poor man not only said he was unclean; he *knew* he was unclean. If he were prone to any illusions, all he had to do was hold what was left of his hand up before his eyes and they vanished in an ugly moment. Moreover, he saw himself as perfectly hopeless. There was nothing he could do to help himself. Everyone else had given up on him too. His many years of illness probably meant that some in his family had discontinued their prayers for him. In this situation, he epitomized the blessed spiritual awareness found in the foundational Beatitudes: "Blessed are the poor in spirit, for theirs is the kingdom of heaven. Blessed are those who mourn, for they shall be comforted" (Matt. 5:3-4).

The piteous refrain, "Unclean! Unclean!" had shaped the leper's whole psyche. He was a beggar indeed. He truly believed that there was nothing within him commendable to God. He was in the perfect posture to receive grace.

God does not come to the self-sufficient, those who think they have no need or imagine that they can make it on their own. He comes to the bankrupt in spirit, those who mourn their condition. It is very probable that the leper had been sitting beyond the range of the crowd, transfixed by Jesus' opening words and the masterful argument that followed, and that the Holy Spirit so overwhelmed him that nothing could keep him from Jesus.

If we would come to Christ, this is the way we must come— saying, "Unclean! Unclean!" In fact, if we come saying "only partly unclean—25 percent clean—10 percent clean," He will not receive us. Have you come to Christ like the leper? It is the only way He receives us and gives the healing touch. That is the first qualification for meeting Christ.

WORSHIPFUL SUBMISSION. The second qualification is in the first sentence of Matthew 8:2: "And behold, a leper came to

Him, *and bowed down to Him"* (italics added). It is worshipful submission. The word used to describe his bowing takes us into the leper's heart. The basic meaning of the word in early Greek literature was "to kiss," as in kissing the earth as one lay prostrate to the gods. In the Old Testament, it was used to translate the Hebrew word for *bowing down*.⁴ Luke tells us he "fell on his face" (Luke 5:2), which enhances the picture. The humble leper put his whole soul into adoration as he lay prostrate before Christ. He worshiped Christ as the only possible source of his healing. The lesson is clear for us. Christ's healing touch doesn't come with a casual, irreverent acknowledgment. It comes as we bow before Him in realization that He is our *only* hope.

REAL FAITH. The third factor in obtaining the healing touch of Christ is faith. The leper demonstrated remarkable faith. The whole of Matthew 8:2 reads, "And behold a leper came to Him, and bowed down to Him, saying, 'Lord if you are willing, you can make me clean.' " Mark indicates that he repeated this several times (Mark 1:40). How poignant the picture is with the leper still prostrate, repeating in the hoarse voice typical of those with advanced leprosy, "Lord, if You are willing, You can make me clean—Lord, if You are willing, You can make me clean." No doubt he had heard of Jesus' miraculous power, had been listening to Him that day, and had come to the conclusion that Christ was omnipotent. Christ had the power. But what is more significant is that the leper said, "You can make *me* clean." He believed that Jesus could save even him. We must all believe this if we are to receive grace.

How do we obtain His healing touch? We recognize our sinful condition; we bow before Him in reverence as the only source of our healing; and we believe that He can do it *for us*.

Experiencing the Healing Touch of Christ

As the leper lay at Jesus' feet, Jesus looked on him as he had never before been viewed. According to Mark's Gospel, Christ was "moved with compassion" (Mark 1:41), indicating that Jesus was so touched by what He saw that He felt it in His stomach. And then came the height of the encounter. "Stretching out His hand, [Jesus] touched him" (Matt. 8:3). Perhaps it had been twenty or even thirty years since the leper had been touched by a nonleprous hand. Perhaps he was a father and had once known the embrace of his children and his wife, but for years he had not known even a touch. Now the touch of Christ—and as Bishop Westcott says, the word "expresses more than superficial contact."[5] It is often translated "to take hold of." Jesus, at the very least, placed His hand firmly on the leper.

How beautiful Christ is. He didn't have to do that. He could have spoken a word or simply willed it. But He chose to lay His hand on the poor man in front of the multitude. The onlookers were shocked. The disciples were shocked. Jesus was now ceremonially unclean—and besides He might catch the disease, they thought. Why did Jesus do it? There are some very human reasons. Reaching out was the reflex of His life. It was the instinct of His loving heart. But He also wanted to clear away any fears the man had. He wanted the leper to *feel* His willingness and sympathy. The touch said, "I'm with you. I understand." Those were the human reasons, but there was an overshadowing theological reason. The touch of His pure hand on the rotting leper is a parable of the Incarnation. Jesus in the Incarnation lay hold of our flesh. He took on flesh, became sin for us, and thus gave us His purity. [God] made [Jesus] who knew no sin to be sin on our behalf, that we might become the righteousness of God in Him" (2 Cor. 5:21). Jesus lay hold of our flesh. He touched us and healed us.

The Miracle

And the healing? Matthew concludes: "And stretching out His hand, He touched him saying, 'I am willing; be cleansed.' And immediately his leprosy was cleansed" (Matt. 8:3). The cleansing was instantaneous. Everyone saw it: the lionized face, the brows, the eyelashes, the nose, the ears, the hair were all instantly restored! The clawlike hands, the stubs he called feet were completely whole. No doubt a thunderous roar rose from the multitude as the realization of what had happened set in. And the leper? We can only guess at how he reacted and what he said. But I surmise it was not "Unclean! Unclean!" but, "I'm clean! I'm clean!" And that is what Jesus Christ can do for you in an instant, in a split second of belief.

The lessons of the leper are three. If you would be healed you must:

1.   Come to Christ with a deep awareness of your sin. Do you now acknowledge that you are a sinner and that you have nothing in yourself to commend you to God? Do you mourn your sin? If so, you are ready for the second step.
2.   Bow before Him in humble reverence. Worship Him as your only hope. And in doing this, move on to the final element.
3.   Believe that He can do it. Say, "Lord, if You are willing, You can make me clean." Believe in Him, and He will touch you right now and you will be cleansed.

If you have not done this, do not read another page until the matter is settled. Right now nothing else matters. Do it!

NOTES

[1]Philip Yancey, *Where Is God When It Hurts?* 1977, Zondervan, p. 32.

[2]William Barclay, *The Gospel of Matthew,* vol. 2, Westminster, 1958, p. 301.

[3]Richard Chenevix Trench, *Notes on the Miracles of Our Lord,* Baker, 1956, p. 135.

[4]Colin Brown, *The New International Dictionary of New Testament Theology,* vol. 2, Zondervan, 1979, pp. 875-877.

[5]Brooke Foss Westcott, *Christian Aspects of Life,* Macmillan, 1897, p. 354.

ELEVEN.
THE RECEIVERS

"Ask, and it shall be given to you; seek, and you shall find; knock, and it shall be opened to you" (Matt. 7:7).

When Howard Carter, the British archeologist, first peered wide-eyed into the ancient Egyptian tomb he had just opened, he saw nothing. The year was 1922. For more than twenty centuries archeologists, tourists, and tomb robbers had searched for the burial places of Egypt's pharaohs. It was believed that nothing remained undisturbed, especially in the Royal Valley where the ancient monarchs had been buried for millennia. With only a few scraps of evidence, Carter carried on his pursuit, personally financed because no one felt there was anything left to be discovered. Somewhere . . . somehow . . . he was convinced that one tomb remained.

Twice during his six-year search he was within two yards of the first stone step leading to the burial chamber. Finally he found it. "Can you see anything?" his assistants asked, as Howard Carter's eyes adjusted to the semidarkness. Carter was seeing, but he had difficulty speaking because he was looking at what no modern man had ever seen. Wooden animals, statues, chests, chariots, carved cobras, vases, daggers, jewels, a throne . . . and a hand-carved coffin of a teenage king. It was, of course, the priceless tomb and treasure of King Tutankhamen, the world's most exciting archeological discovery.

Howard Carter's perseverance is to be applauded, for because of his steadfastness he succeeded where others had failed. In the spiritual realm, such doggedness is even more commendable because it too will bring success where others have failed. Those who learn to ask, seek, and knock will find. And the treasure will far exceed that of King Tut.

Spiritual Treasure

Jesus' words recorded in Matthew 7:7-11 describe the way a man or woman who understands what the Sermon on the Mount is all about will pray. The instruction which Jesus gives on prayer should not be lifted from its context in the Sermon and abused, as is so common today. All of us have heard it done. It goes something like this: the Bible says, "Ask, and it shall be given to you; seek, and you shall find; knock, and it shall be opened to you." Therefore, all we have to do is ask for it with faith and persistence, and we will get it. "You do not have because you do not ask" (James 4:2)—so go for it! "Name it and claim it!" This view sees God as a celestial slot machine. Pull the handle enough times in prayer and you will get what you want.

Such thinking is entirely wrong. A text apart from its context is pretext. So we must refrain from isolating "ask . . . seek . . . knock" from its context, for the context is imminently spiritual. The broad context of the Sermon sets down the surpassing righteousness, humility, sincerity, purity, and love expected of those who are members of the kingdom of God. These virtues are beyond human attainment apart from God's grace. The broad context underscores our spiritual need.

Likewise, the context immediately preceding "ask . . . seek . . . knock" is explicitly spiritual. In Matthew 7:1-6, Jesus has shown us the danger of condemning other people as if we were judges. He also has told us to remove the log from our own eye before attempting to remove the speck from someone else's. His warning is, "For in the way you judge, you will be judged; and by your standard of measure, it will be measured to you" (v. 2). The standard is terrifying. How can we live up to it? The answer: we need to be cleansed. We need God's help and His grace. But from where? And Jesus answers, "Ask, and it shall be given to you; seek, and you shall find; knock, and it shall be opened to you" (v. 7).

This famous text is not a text to apply to our material desires. *It tells us how to pray for the character of the kingdom in our lives.* In respect to the theme of this book, it tells believers how to pray the Beatitudes into their lives.

We Are to Pray with Persistence
Jesus begins with some advice about attitude:

> Ask, and it shall be given to you; seek, and you shall find; knock, and it shall be opened to you. For everyone who asks receives; and he who seeks finds; and to him who knocks it shall be opened (Matt. 7:7-8).

The Lord's language is unusually compelling because the three verbs *ask, seek,* and *knock* indicate an ascending intensity. *Ask* implies requesting assistance for a conscious need. We realize our lack and thus ask for help. The word also suggests humility in asking, for it is commonly used of one asking a superior. The next step, *seek,* involves asking, but adds action. The idea is not just to express our need, but to get up and look around for help. It involves effort. The final step, *knock,* includes asking plus acting plus persevering—like someone who keeps pounding on a closed door!

The stacking of these words is extremely forceful, and the fact that they are present imperatives gives them even more punch. The text actually reads: "Keep on asking, and it shall be given to you; keep on seeking, and you shall find; keep on knocking, and it shall be opened to you." This picture is of a man who will not stop knocking.

INTENSE ASKING. These verses are remarkably intense—and there is no doubt that our Lord meant for them to be understood this way. In one of His prayer parables in the Gospel of Luke, the Lord urges the same intensity:

Now He was telling them a parable to show that at all times they ought to pray and not to lose heart, saying, "There was in a certain city a judge who did not fear God, and did not respect man. And there was a widow in that city, and she kept coming to him, saying, 'Give me legal protection from my opponent.' And for a while he was unwilling; but afterward he said to himself, 'Even though I do not fear God nor respect man, yet because this widow bothers me, I will give her legal protection, lest by continually coming she wear me out.' " And the Lord said, "Hear what the unrighteous judge said" (Luke 18:1-6).

The cultivation of persistence in one's prayer life was evidently a recurring motif in Jesus' teaching on prayer. And here in Matthew 7:7, which is subject to the immense spiritual force of what has been said in the Sermon on the Mount, Christ's point is this: *we are to passionately persist in prayer for the elements of spiritual growth.* We naturally persevere in our prayers when one close to us is ill. Likewise, if we are in financial trouble, or if we are expecting a promotion, or if we have some frightening task ahead of us, we pray intensely.

But the question is: do we persist in our prayers for spiritual growth for ourselves and others? Do we "ask . . . seek . . . knock" for poverty of spirit? Do we keep knocking for a merciful attitude, or for a pure heart, or to be peacemakers? On the whole, most Christians do not. And the reason is they have never understood that in this text Christ is encouraging the pursuit of spiritual things rather than material. Consider what would happen to Christianity if God's people understood what Christ is saying here and put it to work. Think—because we will return to this thought.

INTENSE NEED. Apart from correctly understanding this verse, what it will take to drive us to passionate prayer for our spiritual development is a sensed need for God's grace. First, we see what the kingdom requires as to righteousness. It is perfection (Matt. 5:48). We are to be holy as He is holy (Lev. 19:2). Only the pure in heart shall see God (Matt. 5:8). Then we see ourselves, and we know that though we do good things, we are evil; that all of us, Jews and Greeks, are under sin (Rom. 3:9). The dual sight of His perfect standard and our own sin drives us to our knees and to His grace. We learn that there is no hope for spiritual improvement apart from grace. It is the one who sees this reality who rejoices to read Jesus' invitation to ask, seek, and knock.

Let the text rest heavily upon us. We are to ask and keep on asking for those things which will make us more like Jesus. We are to seek and keep on seeking. We are to knock and keep on knocking. Perseverance is the key to God's treasure, as it has often proved to be in the matters of earthly treasure, as with Howard Carter.

But how much greater our rewards when we persevere in praying for God's treasures. Exaggeration? We think not. King Tut's treasure brought him no happiness; and if we were as rich as he, the effect would be the same. Besides, King Tut left it all behind. The treasure Christ gives is eternally ours and eternally satisfying.

Perhaps we may wonder why it is that God wants us to persist intensely for things which He surely wants to give us. The answer lies with us. He wants to give us all things, but He cannot give them until we are ready. Persistent prayer for them prepares us!

We Are to Pray with Confidence

The last part of Jesus' command teaches us that we are not only to pray with persistence, but with confidence. The verses we have studied shout assurance to us: "Ask, and it shall be given to you; seek, and you shall find; knock, and it shall be opened to you." The only condition for our receiving spiritual treasure is persistence. If we persistently ask, we *will* receive it.

I am grateful this verse is not a blank check for anything in life. I am thankful it cannot be applied to anything we want. Dr. Howard Hendricks recalls that when he was a young man, certain mothers had set their hopes on him in behalf of their daughters. One mother even said to him, "Howard, I just want

you to know that I am praying that you will be my son-in-law."
Says Dr. Hendricks of this, "Have you ever thanked God for
unanswered prayer?" I am grateful that God has not answered all
my prayers too. And so are you. On the other hand, how
wonderful it is that He has always answered our persistent
prayers for spiritual growth.

THE FATHER ANSWERS OUR PRAYERS. Jesus assures us that
this is true with an illustration based on earthly fatherhood:
"What man is there among you, when his son shall ask him for a
loaf, will give him a stone? Or if he shall ask for a fish, he will
not give him a snake, will he?" (Matt. 7:9-10)

The illustration is absurd. The Galileans who first heard it
were familiar with the flat stones on the seashore which looked
exactly like their round, flat cakes of bread; they were also aware
that fish (more likely eels) looked very much like snakes. The
picture is of a son coming to ask his father for something to eat
and his father replying, "Here son, enjoy!" as the boy cracks his
teeth. "Oh, you did not like that. Here, have a fish," and he
gives him a harmful snake or eel. No true father would be as
ignorant or cruel. Fathers give what is good.

The Lord crowns His assurance with the example of the
Heavenly Father's giving: "If you then, being evil, know how to
give good gifts to your children, how much more shall your
Father who is in heaven give what is good to those who ask
Him!" (v. 11) It is the familiar *a fortiori* argument that Jesus is
so fond of. If it is true of the lesser, how much more of the
greater. God is our Father, our *Abba,* our dearest Father *par
excellence!* Think of our earthly fathers at their very best and
multiply their best by infinity and we have it. Isaiah says of the
Father's care, "Can a woman forget her nursing child, and have
no compassion on the son of her womb? Even these may forget,
but I will not forget you" (Isa. 49:15). The "how much more"
of our text has an infinite ring.

THE HOLY SPIRIT ANSWERS OUR PRAYERS. An earthly father
would never give his child a stone for bread, but sometimes he
makes mistakes. Earthly fathers may think they are doing the
right thing only to discover it is absolutely wrong. God never

errs; though in fact, it *is* His policy to give greater quality and quantity than we imagine in our prayers.

Luke's parallel quotation gives us a remarkable insight into the mechanics of God's giving more of "what is good" to those who ask Him. His parallel reads: "If you then, being evil, know how to give good gifts to your children, how much more shall your Heavenly Father give the Holy Spirit to those who ask Him?" (Luke 11:13) Luke's substitution of "Holy Spirit" for "what is good" is no contradiction because it is the Holy Spirit who bestows what is good. Moreover, the Holy Spirit knows what we need better than we do! The Apostle Paul informs us:

> And in the same way the Spirit also helps our weakness; for we do not know how to pray as we should, but the Spirit Himself intercedes for us with groanings too deep for words; and He who searches the hearts knows what the mind of the Spirit is, because He intercedes for the saints according to the will of God (Rom. 8:26-27).

The result is we get more of "what is good" than we ever imagined.

Our assurance is this: if we ask for anything (anything!) that is good for us spiritually, God will give it to us. If you do not have eternal life through Jesus Christ, you may be sure that He will give it to you if you truly ask. If you are a believer but are short on Christian graces, you must ask, and you will receive. If you are untruthful, but are willing to ask, seek, and knock for truthfulness, He will give you the spirit of truth. If you are ungenerous, and will bring this attitude to God in passionate prayer, He will give you a generous spirit. If you are unkind, but will passionately seek God for a kind heart, He will give it to you.

We Must Pray
Now think what would happen if we prayed for our spiritual growth as intensely as we pray for our physical needs? The

church would explode because a far greater proportion of its people would be living kingdom lives. Our pulpits would be filled with preachers of power. The mission fields would shrink as thousands more would pour out to the harvest—with greater power.

PRAY PERSISTENTLY. Do we want the character of the kingdom, the Beautiful Attitudes, in our lives? Then, we have to do two things. First, we must ask persistently. Jesus says we are to "ask and keep on asking; seek and keep on seeking; knock and keep on knocking." We are to beseech God constantly and passionately for spiritual blessing.

PRAY CONFIDENTLY. We are at the same time to ask confidently. Everyone who asks this way receives; and everyone who seeks like this finds; and everyone who knocks and keeps on knocking has it opened to him. God will give us anything we ask for which is good for us spiritually. If we do not have, it is our fault, for as James says, "You do not have because you do not ask" (James 4:2). Over 200 years ago, John Newton wrote about this very thing in one of his great hymns:

Come, my soul, thy case prepare;
Jesus loves to answer prayer;
He Himself has bid thee pray,
Therefore will not say thee nay.

Thou art coming to a King;
Large petitions with thee bring;
For His grace and power are such,
None can ever ask too much.

We can never ask too much spiritually. Let us ask and receive.

Someone once said, "Any discussion of the doctrine of prayer which does not issue in the practice of prayer is not only *not* helpful, but harmful." It is true. If God is speaking to you, you must pray.

First, single out the spiritual qualities which you would like to cultivate. In reference to the Beatitudes, it may be poverty of spirit or meekness or purity of heart. Write them on your prayer list and begin to regularly pray.

Second, as you pray, pray persistently—asking, seeking, knocking. Seek them with all your being.

Third, know this: that you *will* receive them. And they will be better than you have dreamed, because your Heavenly Father will give them to you. You will be blessed, because He will call you "blessed."

```
┌─────────────────────┐
│                     │
│     BECOMING        │
│        A            │
│     BLESSING        │
│                     │
└─────────────────────┘
```

What happens when the Beautiful Attitudes are not only rooted, but flourish in our lives? The Lord Jesus answers this question by framing the Beatitudes with two brilliant metaphors.

First, *salt:* "You are the salt of the earth; but if the salt has become tasteless, how will it be made salty again? It is good for nothing anymore, except to be thrown out and trampled under foot by men" (Matt. 5:13).

Second, *light:* "You are the light of the world. A city set on a hill cannot be hidden. Nor do men light a lamp, and put it under the peck-measure, but on the lampstand; and it gives light to all who are in the house. Let your light shine before men in such a way that they may see your good works, and glorify your Father who is in heaven" (Matt. 5:14-16).

Lord, make the Beatitudes grow in us so that we may be salt to a decaying world, and light in the midst of darkness. Amen.

TWELVE.
THE SALT

"You are the salt of the earth; but if the salt has become tasteless, how will it be made salty again? It is good for nothing anymore, except to be thrown out and trampled under foot by men" (Matt. 5:13).

Realizing that the Beatitudes are essentially interior, one might be tempted to think that they can be lived in isolation, away from the contradictory world. But it is just the opposite. It is impossible to live these eight characteristics of the kingdom in private. They are powerfully social and outward when put to work. And that is why Christ crowns them with two brilliant and searching metaphors (those of salt and light), which tell us how those who live the Beatitudes must relate to the world.

Knowing the situation as we do, that Christ had only a few poor, uneducated followers, His words no doubt appeared to some as presumptuous and even absurd. "You, you alone, are the salt of the earth—not just Palestine, but the whole earth." The Lord was saying that His followers would perform a universal task that would affect all mankind. He was expressing a mysterious confidence. Stranger still, we know that they ultimately did it, despite their shortcomings and inconsistencies.

As we study the church's mission through the medium of the metaphor of salt, we will consider the salted church, the desalted church, and the resalted church.

115

The Salted Church

What did Jesus mean by, "You are the salt of the earth"? Fundamental to understanding His statement is the fact that in the ancient world the primary function of salt was as a preservative. There were no ice-making machines in the first century. Refrigeration was beyond man's wildest dreams. The only way to preserve meat was to salt it down or soak it in a saline solution. In fact, this was common practice right into the 20th century in remote areas of the world. It was particularly the experience of pioneer missionaries. As one describes it:

> This was absolutely imperative. Under the high temperatures and hot weather of the region, decay and decomposition of meat was astonishingly rapid. We had no winter weather, or cool, frosty nights to chill the flesh. Besides this, swarms of ubiquitous flies soon hovered over the butchered carcasses. The only way to prevent them from ruining the meat . . . was to soak the slabs of meat in a strong solution of salt.[1]

As a matter of historical interest, this preserving quality of salt was what made it possible for David Livingstone's body to be shipped back to England for interment in Westminster Abbey. Having died in deepest Africa, Livingstone's servant buried the great missionary's heart in African soil, and then salted his body and shipped it home for an honored burial. Understanding that salt is a preservative is fundamental to understanding Jesus' words.

THE SALTED CHURCH, A PRESERVATIVE. Realizing this, the negative implication of "You are the salt of the earth" is that the world tends toward rot and decomposition. Jesus was under no illusion about the world apart from Himself. When the world is left to itself, it tends to fester and putrify, for the germs of evil are everywhere present and active. This is the consistent teaching of Scripture and biblical history. The world was a perfect creation, but sin came and decay set in, with the result that it became so rotten that God removed virtually the entire population by the Flood. Given another chance, there was immediate debauchery—and with time came Sodom and Gomorrah. We live in a world that constantly tends toward decay. Some of the Christless structures of the world may look OK on the outside, but inside they are rotting away.

The church, as salt, functions as a retardant to decay in a disintegrating world. Jesus says in effect: "Humanity without Me is a dead body that is rotting and falling apart. And, you, My followers, are the salt which must be rubbed into the flesh to halt the decomposition." The church must be rubbed into the world—into its rotting flesh and wounds that it might be preserved.

This matter of being a preservative has positive and negative aspects. On the negative side, the presence of a salty Christian will retard decay, simply because his or her life is a reproach to the sin of those around. We all know that there are certain people in whose presence a filthy story is naturally told, and that there are others before whom no one would think of telling such a story. It is not because the salty Christian is self-righteous or condemning, but rather because his or her life is such a witness that evil conversation seems shabby and inappropriate.

Such Christians exert an incalculable influence on society. Their presence reduces crime, restrains ethical corruption, promotes honesty, quickens the conscience, and elevates the general moral atmosphere. The presence of such people in the military, in business, in education, in a fraternity or sorority will amazingly elevate the level of living. And their absence will allow unbelievable depths of depravity. Believers, salty believers, are the world's perservative. The question we must ask ourselves is, what happens when we get to know people who are without Christ? Does our presence make a difference for them? Are we salt?

There is also the positive aspect. Not only are our lives meant to reprove evil, but they are also meant to elicit the best from those about us. What a beautiful thought. Sad to say, not everyone who claims to be a Christian has this effect. Henrik Ibsen, in one of his plays, put this complaint on the lips of the

Roman Emperor Julian:

> Have you looked at these Christians closely? Hollow-
> eyed, pale-cheeked, flat-breasted all; they brood their
> lives away, unspurred by ambition: the sun shines for
> them, but they do not see it: the earth offers them its
> fullness, but they desire it not; all their desire is to
> renounce and to suffer that they may come to die.[2]

John Keats gave his estimation of Christianity by writing: "Thou
hast conquered, O pale Galilean." Oliver Wendell Holmes put it
this way: "I might have entered the ministry if certain clergymen
I knew had not acted and looked so much like undertakers."

THE SALTED CHURCH, A SPICE. That's not the way true salted
Christians are. Rather, that is the way life is without Christ. Life
without Christ is insipid and dull. That is why our culture
attempts to numb itself with pleasure and drugs. People are
literally dying of boredom. The entertainment industry does its
best to make it look otherwise. Fictional good is made out to be
boring and flat, while fictional evil is portrayed as exciting and
intriguing; but it is the other way around. As Simone Weil says,
"Nothing is so beautiful, nothing so continually fresh and surprising, so full of sweet and perpetual ecstasy, as the good: no
desert is so dreary, monotonous, and boring as evil.[3]

In biblical times, as today, salt was not only a preservative,
but a spice, a condiment. Christianity is what brings spice and
zest to life. The bland is made savory; the unpalatable becomes a
delight. Believers must be salty, not only because they are
righteous, but because life is alive. They ought to write the best
books, be the most courteous, work the hardest, be the best
musicians and artists, craftsmen and students.

THE SALTED CHURCH CREATES THIRST. All of this anticipates
another result of being salty—and that is that salt creates thirst.
Jesus made people thirsty for God the Father. Whenever anyone
encountered Jesus, be he a Pharisee like Nicodemus or an outcast
like Mary Magdalene, that person was made to thirst. Are we
salty enough to make people thirsty for Jesus?

When we sit down for dinner, one bite is enough to know whether the food has been salted or not. Just a pinch of salt goes a long way. William Wilberforce, the man who almost single-handedly brought about the slavery Emancipation Bill in England, is living proof of this. Dwarfed by disease, he did not appear to be much. However, James Boswell wrote of him, after listening to one of his speeches, "I saw a shrimp mount the table; but as I listened, he grew and grew until the shrimp became a whale."[4] Tiny, elfish, misshapen, he was salt to British society, not only bringing preservation but enticement to Christ by his beautiful life. A little salt will make its presence felt.

The Desalted Church

Our Lord indicates the possibility of a desalted church with the words, "if the salt has become tasteless." In actuality, salt is an extremely stable compound and does not become tasteless. The consensus of scholars is that Jesus is referring to its adulteration or dilution. The fact is, it is dangerously easy for Christians to become diluted and lose their salty, preserving influence in the world. While many believers are pungent and salty, there are others who are virtually indistinguishable from the surrounding culture. We cannot look at Christianity at large, or American Christianity, or local Christianity, or at our own hearts, without admitting that the possibility of saltless, insipid, bland Christianity is very real.

If we are not affecting the world, the world is affecting us. We are to export our influence to those around us, but if there are more imports than exports—if there are greater influences coming in than going out—we will become like the world. If we are not salting the world, the world is rotting us. The great tragedy is that so often the world does the church more harm than the church does the world good.

We must ask ourselves if there is any difference between our approach to materialism and that of the world. Are there any distinctions between our approach to pleasure and the world's? Do we approach happiness differently? Is there a difference in our ethics? Does our compassion fit within the limitations of the world? The answers to these questions will reveal whether the salt is salty, or if it has been desalted.

The Resalted Church
Is there hope for a desalted church? The Lord brings up this question by saying, "How will it [salt] be made salty again?" As we have seen, salt cannot *lose* its saltiness, and so here we must affirm that it cannot be *made* salty. In the context of His times, Christ is saying that if salt has lost its savor (has been diluted), there is no *natural* hope for it. Is there any natural hope for us if we have lost our savor by worldly dilution? The answer is no. However, Jesus extends the metaphor into the supernatural and here we must answer yes! Jesus is not teaching that if a Christian loses his pungency, he cannot get it back. Nothing but our own sin can keep us from being restored—resalted.

I have an acquaintance who in his sixties was resalted. His Christian life had become bland and insipid. But God graciously confronted him with his condition and the necessity of a vital, salty life, and he committed his life to Christ. The last ten years of his life he has had an incredibly salty effect on the world. His life has touched thousands. So the church can be resalted.

There is an urgency in what Jesus has to say, and it is found in the concluding sentence of Matthew 5:13 where He warns of the destiny of saltless salt: "It is good for nothing anymore, except to be thrown out and trampled under foot by men." Since it is useless, it will be tossed onto the road where perhaps it will fill in a few cracks and be further adulterated. It will sterilize the soil, retard plant growth, and make barren the surroundings. This substance, so beneficial to life in its pungent, pure form, brings desolation when cast aside. This is the sad parable of the Christian life that has lost its saltiness. It is good for nothing at all.

Such is the testimony of church history. We search in vain for the once-great church of Asia Minor with its flourishing parishes. The churches of Corinth and Ephesus are all but nonexistent. We look in vain for the church of North Africa where the great Augustine ministered. Salt that lost its saltiness was cast out and trodden under foot by the men of the world.

Be Salt
Yet despite the church's failures, Christ's use of this metaphor is boldly positive. Jesus says, "You (you alone) are the salt of the earth." Jesus believes in us. He is optimistic. Jesus believes that we can have a healing, preserving influence on our own society and the world. He believes that we can bring flavor to life—that we can make the world thirsty for Him. And the church has done just that again and again.

We are salt! Christ wants us to cultivate our saltiness by constantly communing with Him and being constantly filled with the Spirit. Then He wants us to get out of the salt shaker into the world—even rubbing ourselves into its rotting wounds. And He wants us to remember that though we are not much, "a little salt goes a long way!"

NOTES

[1]W. Phillip Keller, *Salt for Society,* Word, 1981, p. 100.
[2]William Barclay, *The Gospel of Matthew,* vol. 2, Westminster, 1958, p. 116.
[3]Malcolm Muggeridge, *Christ and the Media,* Eerdmans, 1977, p. 46.
[4]F.W. Boreham, *A Bunch of Everlastings,* Abingdon, 1920, p. 186.

THIRTEEN.
THE LIGHT

"You are the light of the world. A city set on a hill cannot be hidden. Nor do men light a lamp and put it under the peck-measure, but on the lampstand; and it gives light to all who are in the house. Let your light shine before men in such a way that they may see your good works, and glorify your Father who is in heaven" (Matt. 5:14-16).

The story of how Jesus identified Himself as the "light of the world" is remarkably beautiful and instructive. It happened on the day following the spectacular nighttime ceremony known as the Illumination of the Temple. The Illumination of the Temple took place in the temple treasury before four massive golden candelabra topped with huge torches. It is said that the candelabra were as tall as the highest walls of the temple, and that at the top of these candelabra were mounted great bowls which held sixty-five liters of oil. There was a ladder for each candelabrum, and when the evening came, healthy young priests would carry oil up to the great bowls and light the protruding wicks. Eyewitnesses said that the huge flames which leapt from these torches illuminated not only the temple but all of Jerusalem. The Mishna tells us that,

> Men of piety and good works used to dance before them [the candelabra] with burning torches in their hands singing songs and praises and countless Levites played on harps, lyres, cymbals, and trumpets and instruments of music.[1]

123

The exotic rite celebrated the great pillar of fire (the glorious cloud of God's presence) which led the Israelites during their sojourn in the wilderness and spread its fiery billows over the tabernacle.

It was in the temple treasury the following morning, with the charred torches still in place, that Jesus lifted His voice above the crowd and proclaimed, "I am the light of the world." There could scarcely be a more emphatic way to announce one of the supreme truths of His existence. Christ was saying in effect, "The pillar of fire that came between you and the Egyptians, the cloud that guided you by day in the wilderness and illumined the night and enveloped the tabernacle, the glorious cloud that filled Solomon's temple—was Me!" "I am the light of the world; he who follows Me shall not walk in the darkness, but shall have the light of life" (John 8:12). Jesus is the light of the world! He is everything suggested by the storied cloud of glory. And He is everything suggested by the sublime metaphor of light—and much more.

The immense truth that Christ is the light of the world must be foundational to our thinking, and indeed, must control it, as we now take up the unforgettable words of Matthew 5:14-16 where He applies the metaphor to *us*.

The World Is in Darkness

The fundamental truth that Jesus is the light of the world is indeed a glorious one, but it suggests the equally foundational but inglorious truth that the world is in darkness. The darkness is a spiritual darkness which dominates the entire world system, and it is terrible. But the real horror is that the inhabitants of the earth love it. John wrote, "And this is the judgment, that light is come into the world, and men loved the darkness rather than the light; for their deeds were evil" (John 3:19). Darkness by itself is one thing, but intentional darkness is far worse. To be subject to the darkness of the night before the dawn is one thing, but it is quite another thing to deliberately live down in the earth among the caves and the bats, refusing to come to the light.

Why this preference for darkness? John tells us that the world loves darkness because its deeds are evil. Unconsciously, and sometimes consciously, the world reasons very much like Lady Macbeth as she planned a murder:

'Com, thick night, and pall thee in the dunnest smoke of hell, that my keen knife see not the wound it makes, nor heaven peep through the blanket of the dark.[2]

It is a grim, unhappy picture; but it is biblical and therefore true. The world is in darkness.

We Are Light

It is the reality of the world's darkness that makes Jesus' pronouncement so thrilling. "You (you alone) are the light of the world." If we are truly believers, we are the light of the world. To say such a thing about ourselves without divine precedent and sanction would be the height of arrogance. But Christ says it, and it is easily one of the most amazing statements to ever fall from His lips—especially realizing what we are like. It is a fact: we are light.

How can this possibly be? Dr. Donald Grey Barnhouse, the master of illustration, explained it this way: when Christ was in the world, He was like the shining sun which is here in the day and gone at night. When the sun sets, the moon comes up; and the moon is a picture of the believers, or the church. The church shines but it does not shine with its own light. It shines with *reflected* light. When Jesus was in the world He said, "I am the light of the world." But as He contemplated leaving the world, He told His disciples, "You are the light of the world." At times the church has been a full moon dazzling the world with an almost daytime light. These have been times of great enlightenment, such as those of Paul and Luther and Wesley. And at other times the church has been only a thumbnail moon—and very little light shines on the earth. But whether the church is a full moon or a new thumbnail moon, waxing or waning, it reflects the light of the sun.[3] Our light is a reflected or derived light. It does not originate from us.

HOW MYSTERIOUS. However, the Scriptures teach that our light is more than reflected; we, in fact, *become* light ourselves. The Apostle Paul said, "For you were formerly darkness, but now you are light in the Lord; walk as light" (Eph. 5:8). Somehow our incorporation in Christ allows us to some extent to *be* light—however imperfect. Our light is still derived from Him—not a ray of it comes from ourselves—but it is more than reflected. We have been made "partakers of the divine nature," as Peter says (2 Peter 1:4). It is a mystery.

But the beautiful thing is, mystery that it is, it works! The church has had some great shining lights. When the English martyrs Hugh Latimer and Nicholas Ridley were being taken to the stake for burning, Latimer turned to Ridley and said, "Be of good cheer, Brother Ridley, we have lighted such a candle in England as by the grace of God shall never be put out." Latimer and Ridley continue to burn as great lights in the world.

There are also lesser lights, for the mystery works for all believers, even children. When my now-grown daughter, Holly, was in kindergarten, she weekly approached her teacher, Mrs. Smith, and timidly said, "Mrs. Smith, will you come to church?" Mrs. Smith would promise to attend. And when Mrs. Smith didn't show, Holly would again approach Mrs. Smith on Monday morning and say, "Mrs. Smith, you didn't come to church." Who could resist those big, sad, brown eyes? Finally Mrs. Smith came, and she came again, and she came to know Jesus. And today she is a remarkable, radiant sunbeam herself. It is a mystery, and it is beautiful. The facts are: first, Jesus is the light; second, the world is in darkness; and third, somehow believers are light. Believers shine.

HOW TO SHINE. Seeing that we are light, how can we shine more? The answer is in this story. A man returning from a journey brought his wife a matchbox that would glow in the dark. After giving it to her she turned out the light, but the matchbox could not be seen. Both thought they had been cheated. Then the wife noticed some French words on the box and called a friend to translate. And this is what the inscription said:

"If you want me to shine in the night, keep me in the light." So it is with us! We must expose ourselves to Jesus, revel in His Word, spend time in prayer soaking up His rays. As Paul wrote, "But we all, with unveiled face beholding as in a mirror the glory of the Lord, are being transformed into the same image from glory to glory, just as from the Lord, the Spirit" (2 Cor. 3:18). If you want to shine in the night, keep your eye on the Light.

The Spiritual Function of Light in the World

Turning us from the spiritual *facts* of light to its *function* in this world, Jesus presents two scenes: a city perched on a hill and a light set in a home.

AS CITIES ON HILLS. First, believers are to function like a city set on a hill. Jesus says, "A city set on a hill cannot be hidden" (Matt. 5:14). There is no way to obscure a city on the crest of a hill. Having stayed in Ecuador, I can testify that the light of the city of Quito, situated at 10,000 feet above sea level, illumines the sky for 75 miles around. It cannot be hidden. Yet when one is in the great city itself, the lights from the tiny villages even higher above in the Andes are easily seen as well. Cities on hills cannot be hidden. Believers are like this. They are visible. As Martyn Lloyd-Jones said, "If we find in ourselves a tendency to put the light under a bushel, we must begin to examine ourselves and make sure that it really is light."[4] It is good advice, gracious advice! The question is: do we hide our light? And, if so, are we really light? Christians are visible, and this visibility makes them like the beckoning lights of a city on a hill. Inside there is light and what goes with it—warmth and safety.

AS HOUSEHOLD LAMPS. In addition to being like a hilltop city, believers are like an ancient household lamp. Jesus says, "Nor do men light a lamp, and put it under the peck-measure, but on the lampstand; and it gives light to all who are in the house" (Matt. 5:15). The point is unmistakable, for the principal function of a household lamp, and thus a believer, is to provide illumination. Here the simple metaphor tells us so much:

Light reveals things as they really are. All of us have at some time walked into an unfamiliar room and have felt our way to the lamp and turned on the light, discovering a room far different from what we imagined.

Light promotes life. We all know that our summer patio plants will flourish in the basement during winter if we provide them with enough light—even if it is artificial. Even our broken bones mend faster if we can soak up some sunlight. Light is life-giving.

Light is persistent. It constantly assaults the surface of the earth and will penetrate the slightest crack. The darkest place is not safe from it if the tiniest opening appears. So it is with Christ's light.

Light awakens. Have you ever heard the sun rise? Actually, we all have. In a quiet place in the country we can hear the sun rise as it calls nature awake. This is the way it is with spiritual light.

As lamps, the Divine Householder places us strategically. "Nor do men light a lamp, and put it under the peck-measure but on a lampstand." The light is placed so it can shine to its best advantage. We are simply to shine where we have been placed. In fact, in the darker and less promising places our light may have the greatest effect. Like that of Dr. Boris Kornfeld who shared his faith with the diseased and sickly Aleksandr Solzhenitsyn in the Russian gulag.[5] God is in accord with the familiar Gospel tune which commands, "Brighten the corner where you are." It might be good right now to stop and commit the corners to God.

God has made us *visible* like a city on a hill, and He has made us to *illumine* life like a lamp in a dark room. He has placed us where He knows we can shine to His best advantage. Our presence is to reveal life, sin, and goodness as it is, and to provide a light that draws others to it like a summer lamp.

The Spiritual Responsibility Light Brings

The *fact* and *function* of light in our lives brings a vast responsibility. Our Lord is explicit about this: "Let your light shine before men in such a way that they may see your good works, and glorify your Father who is in heaven" (Matt. 5:15). It is a command, not a suggestion. With urgency in His voice, Christ says, "If you are light, then shine!" Let us keep the emotion of this imperative before us!

The medium of shining, He tells us, is our "good works." The word He uses is *kalos* which bears the idea of attractiveness or beauty, rather than the more common *agathos* which means "good in quality." Jesus wants our light to shine through beautiful, attractive works. Of course, He is not recommending self-conscious, staged works. Yet He does suggest that if our works are seen, then let them be beautiful. Our Lord would thus tell us that acts of compassion and caring are at the top of the list. John Stott says it well:

> Indeed, the primary meaning of "works" must be practical, visible deeds of compassion. It is when people see these, Jesus said, that they will glorify God, for they embody the good news of His love which we proclaim. Without them our Gospel loses its credibility and our God His honor.[6]

And why should we be given to beautiful, shining works? Jesus' answer is crystal clear: that they may "glorify your Father who is in heaven." All glory to God! *Soli Deo Gloria.* As David said, "Not to us, O Lord, not to us, but to Thy name give glory" (Ps. 115:1). That is our prayer.

TO SHINE LIKE CHRIST. Jesus' pronouncement, "You (you alone) are the light of the world," is thrilling. It suggests that we can become like Him in relation to this world. We would not have dared to say it, but He did—to our everlasting amazement.

As light, part of Him, we are sure to prevail. Ultimately He will completely vanquish the forces of darkness.

> As by the sun in splendor
> The flags of night are furled,
> So darkness will surrender
> To Christ who lights the world.[7]

TO SHINE FOREVER. Moreover, in eternity we will be part of the light ourselves. Jesus said at the end of the Mystery Parables, "The righteous will shine forth as the sun in the kingdom of their Father" (Matt. 13:43). That is us—you and me! C.S. Lewis once noted that the heavens only reflect the glory of God. But we share the glory of the Father with Christ. And we shall be more glorious than the heavens.

> Nature is mortal. We shall outlive her. When all the suns and nebulae have passed away, each one of you will still be alive. Nature is only the image, the symbol. . . . We are summoned to pass in through nature beyond her to the splendor which she fitfully reflects.[8]

As Christians there is a glory awaiting us that involves, in some mysterious way, shining. We do not know how it will be. Somehow we are going to enter into the fame and approval of God, and we will be glorious beings, far beyond all imagination.

TO SHINE NOW. But right now Jesus says, "You (you alone) are the light of the world." Let us covenant with all our being to shine as brightly as possible in this dark world. Let us covenant to expose ourselves to the face of Jesus in prayer. Let us covenant to be visible for Him. Let us covenant to shine where He has placed us. Let us covenant to do beautiful works. Let us covenant to live the Beautiful Attitudes.

NOTES

[1]*The Mishna,* Sukkah 5:2-3, Herbert Danby, trans., Oxford, 1974, p. 180.
[2]Shakespeare, *Macbeth,* act 1, sc. 5, lines 55-58.
[3]James M. Boice, *The Sermon on the Mount,* Zondervan, 1972, p. 80.
[4]D. Martyn Lloyd-Jones, *Studies in the Sermon on the Mount,*

Vol. 1, Eerdmans, 1959, p. 174.
[5]Charles Colson, *Loving God*, Zondervan, 1983, pp. 27-34.
[6]John R.W. Stott, *The Message of the Sermon on the Mount*, InterVarsity, 1979, p. 62.
[7]James Hastings, ed., *Speaker's Bible*, vol. 6, 1971, p. 108.
[8]C.S. Lewis, *The Weight of Glory*, Eerdmans, 1965, p. 13.